AF594405

This book is dedicated

To the nurturers
To the keepers of ritual
To mothers

To our kin

Kindred

Recipes, spices & rituals to nourish your kin

MARIA & EVA KONECSNY
FOUNDERS OF GEWÜRZHAUS

CONTENTS

Rituals

Introduction

We were born in a little village in the south of Germany, where people still walk to the bakery for bread every morning. Across the sleepy street on which our home stood was a farmhouse and a working barn, and above our terraced garden and through the back gate, horses grazed in the fields. Farm animals outnumbered residents, and everyone knew everyone. It was a wonderful place.

It was there – before we even knew it – that the rituals of seasonality, celebration and family began to seep into our bones. The townspeople picked cherries from their trees in summer, to bottle, or ferment for *Schnaps*. They foraged for mushrooms in autumn, as the leaves dropped in the beautiful mixed forests surrounding the village. In the snow-covered winters, they knit jumpers and stoked their fires. Spring saw everything burst into life, and then, the highlight of the year – the *Dorffest* (village festival), where the community came together to organise, prepare, bake and cook, and to celebrate.

When we moved to Australia only a few years later, we left behind these rhythms, traditions and all of our extended family, in the way that expats often must. This move was the first of many uprootings – we would live in three continents and many more places before we saw out our school years. Yet the promise and the grounding of those early years stayed with us – albeit not always on the surface. Our mother did her best to bring ritual and rhythm to our lives as we moved with Dad's work; she had – and still has – a love for nature, which she used to connect us to each new place.

Perhaps the thing we are most grateful to her for, looking back now, was that she took us to Germany every year for three months, to celebrate Christmas, to spend time with our relatives – to go home. The regularity of these trips steadied us, connecting us not only to our heritage, but also to the ground on which we were born, its smell and taste and texture so different to our new home in Australia. It was there that Mum showed us how it felt to be deeply connected to a place; as much as she loved Australia, her love for Germany was a different kind of love. There, we saw her unencumbered by language and culture, free in the way you feel when you are inherently understood, when you belong. She showed us our place of birth in the best possible way – alive, inspired, in complete and utter love – and she, more than anyone, nurtured our German heritage throughout our childhood.

During those trips back to Germany, we visited family and our parents' long-time friends, and over the years, these visits became rituals. We were nurtured and celebrated, in the way only rarely-seen people are. The place we visited the most was our Oma's tiny apartment on the *Steinberg* in Goslar, where she lived with our great-grandmother, Oma Rosa. A few flights upstairs lived her sister, our great-aunt Babi, and across the road through a big, rambling garden lived her other sister, our great-aunt Dori. We were often dropped off at Oma's for weeks and looked after by these four women. With the snow-covered streets keeping us largely indoors, they taught us how to bake and cook the food of their heritage.

Up with the sun and never idle, our Oma, her sisters and our great-grandmother shaped their days around what was to be produced in the kitchen. If walnuts were on special, we would rug up in our winter coats and briskly walk the distance into town – about half an hour down the hill and through the fortified walls into the historic town centre. There, we made our purchases with the little money our grandmother presided over in her lifetime, then made our way back to her geranium-filled apartment. This path, perhaps more than any other in the world, became home. We walked either side of our Oma, and she would hold our little hands securely. The walk ahead was known, the air was crisp and oftentimes filled with falling snowflakes, and squirrels jumped out ahead of us across the white landscape.

Back in the kitchen, the women taught us all manner of dishes – *Gulasch*, *Ischler*, noodles, potato soup. We watched and learnt. Baking was their favourite thing, the cookies and slices stored in biscuit tins atop our Oma's wardrobe for lack of space. They didn't experiment with food; they made the same things, over and over, the things they grew up eating. For them, after a lifetime of loss and trauma, cooking these foods helped them to hold on to their past in a way that was healing and connecting. Because in food and its gathering, they could remember what sustained them and brought their family around the table.

The Birth of Gewürzhaus

Back in Australia, we moved through our lives. We finished high school, then university after gap years working several bar jobs in Sydney and on a cattle station in the Kimberley. We then took day jobs for a few years before embarking on our first venture together, taking after our entrepreneurial parents – buying, renovating and selling residential houses across rural Australia, as our mother had done through our high school years. We negotiated, painted, installed kitchens and bathrooms, landscaped – anything and everything. After three years, however, the global financial crisis hit and soon after, the banks started knocking back our lending requests. We faced a conundrum: we would have to return to normal jobs to continue in real estate or find a new adventure.

Unsure of our future, we headed back to Germany on a holiday, where our old family friend, Helga, shepherded us through the streets of Munich to a spice shop. We spent over an hour inside, completely in love with the aromas, range and promise of the store. Sitting outside that store with Mum afterwards, we decided that this would be our next venture – to bring self-scoop spices to Melbourne in a beautiful retail setting that would be inspiring and sensorily immersive. It was later during that holiday, watching projector slides from Mum's childhood, that we stumbled upon our grandfather's handwriting. Instinctively, we knew that this should shape the brand we were about to build. The actual script as much as what it symbolised – timelessness, kin, a love of detail. Our Oma's tiny galley kitchen was our other inspiration – we wanted our customers to feel as we did when we spent time there: nurtured, loved, at home and inspired to cook and bake. And so, we came up with the name Gewürzhaus – *Gewürz* meaning spice, *Haus* meaning house. It was daring – and perhaps uncommercial – in its foreignness, but purposefully so: we wanted the name to hold us to account in the long term. To remind us of our beginnings, to remain humble, and generous in our giving, and to nurture as we were nurtured.

Within a year of that holiday, after countless hours of research, blend developing, recipe testing and business planning, we opened our first Gewürzhaus store together with Mum, but not without a steep uphill battle. Despite our property credentials, we were rejected by real estate agents time and again – 'a spice shop?!'. Few saw the potential in our idea – not even Dad – and our lack of traditional retail experience didn't help us convince those pulling the strings. Undeterred, we decided to buy a flailing gelati shop smack bang where we wanted to open our first store – the iconic Lygon Street in Carlton, Melbourne. There was one condition of the lease – if the spice shop failed, we had to promise to revert the store to the current ice cream shop. We laughed this off and signed away – there was no doubt in our minds that our spice shop was going to be successful; we had a clear picture in our heads and hearts of what it would be. And so, we sacrificed our summer to making gelati in an effort to recoup the purchase costs of the business, working on our spice concept in the hours between churning and scooping ice cream. They were long and hard days, and we were exhausted. But by Easter 2010, a year after that all-important trip to Munich, we were ready to close Crema Gelato and open Gewürzhaus.

From day one, the shop was a hit. Our customers were ecstatic; they loved our store and dragged in their friends, who did the same in turn. We were celebrated by every visitor. Perhaps the loveliest thing was that our customers felt inspired to go home and cook. We even had patrons returning with goods they had baked with our spices, wanting to thank us for our advice and existence. This first year was deeply gratifying – we talked to many customers, selling the blends we had made by hand out the back of the store from the whole spices we were sourcing from around the world. We sold about 80 spice blends and many more single-origin spices back then. We were making our own way in the world of retail, ignoring the rules and expectations. At the core, we were doing that by just focusing on connecting with people – through our product and knowledge, through the ambience of our store and through the oftentimes personal conversations we had with our customers. A genuine regard for food and service was our secret ingredient.

Fast forward to today, and despite the significant growth of the business, we are proud that it is still humming the same tune: connection, care and food always at the centre of what we do. We employ many people who share in our mission: to create inspiration to nurture cooking at home for generations to come. This is perhaps our biggest success: that we created a company based on the values instilled in us as children, and that there are many others who share these values, understanding that what we do is so much more than selling a product. Throughout our years as business women, we have learnt a paradigm-shifting lesson: that business is best when governed by the rules of human relationship – decency, honesty, respect, care.

At home, we are also mothers of young children, in whom we try to instil our love of food by role modelling. When we bake with our children, we try to take our time. We chat about technique, how to roll out dough, how much they are allowed to dip their fingers into the bowl. Sometimes, we talk about the ingredients we use, for example the fruit we've picked together from the garden. They ask about our Oma when we use her old mixer or poppy seed mill and we tell them the stories of when we were kids, sticking our fingers into bowls. And so, the cake we bake together, when we share it afterwards, it is so much more than just cake. It's filled with our essence and that makes it deeply nourishing and important to the continuity of life. That is the promise of this book.

Throughout these pages, you will find recipes largely from our heritage, almost always enhanced with spices. Some were handed down to us, most are our take on dishes we ate as children or that are important to our food lines. And a few, like Eva's Crunchy Chilli Oil (page 34), were just too dang good to not share with you. We hope you find joy in their preparation and their sharing. Our hope is that food, when honoured and respected, might nurture us for many more generations.

On Rituals

Have you ever considered what would happen if you took the birthday cake out of a birthday celebration? Those precious moments when family and friends huddle together around the table once a year to sing happy birthday, all focusing on the flickering candles, distractions set aside, the birthday charge's excitement in being the centre of that collective energy – of being celebrated. What would happen if we removed that ritual?

Although the birthday celebration remains a strong ritual in our modern society, so many other traditions, rituals and celebrations have gone by the wayside as our lives become busier and more disconnected from the cycles of our natural world. Time is all-consuming – we are completely controlled by minutes and hours, constantly feeling the inherent pressure of measuring life in this way. Yet time is not created by humans. It originates in the cycles of nature – of the moon and sun, of our days and seasons. There is peace and reassurance to be found here. Because no matter what life throws your way, the moon will show herself again at night, and the sun will light up the next day, and the condition of life will continue – at least that is our hope.

Rituals and celebrations bring us back to these cycles of life. Birthdays, Easter, Christmas and seasonal rituals, like foraging for mushrooms or making sauerkraut – they break up our year into meaningful practices. They help to get you out of your head and into your heart and body. Rituals help us to mark time, stepping out of the day-to-day to honour life by pausing to reflect on it. We practise them in cycles and anticipating their arrival is part of their promise. Sometimes, they bring us together. Other times, they connect us to our surroundings. At other times again, they are the rituals and traditions our ancestors observed, and we continue to carry out. Always, they are symbolic of the cycle of life. Whether that's the celebration of a literal life or the coming and going – the birth and death – of the seasons. There's a constant ebb and flow; one thing comes, another thing goes. By observing and honouring these changes, we are reminded that we are part of something that is bigger than the individual. We are reminded of what we knew so well as children – that life is all around us: precious, magical and to be lived in this moment.

Cooking and baking, in themselves, are age-old rituals. The proverbial dining table and kitchen are places we all gather around, no matter where we are from. These places are a sacred communal space in which we cook and share our lives through conversation – often the only time we stop and do so throughout the day. When you cook to feed your kin, know and draw meaning from the fact that you are connected in the present to a thread running back through time. A thread that you will pass along to future generations, consciously or unconsciously. And, know that all of us have this, even if we haven't realised; we have cultural heritage. There is ritual in our lineage. Find this and you can draw enormous meaning and grounding from it. As our photographer, Amy, once put it so beautifully, 'Don't underestimate how important your knowledge and traditions are for bringing people together'.

Ritual doesn't always need to be elaborate or grand – it can be a big cultural tradition, like the celebration of Christmas, or it can be a much simpler family ritual, like putting on a pot of marmalade when the first oranges drop from your tree. It can be marking an anniversary with a rose of the same colour every year. We encourage you to explore and experiment: find the rituals that come naturally – and bring meaning – to you and your family. Don't be afraid of putting your own spin on things and don't feel pressure – it is not a performance. All you have to do is honour them with your time, attention and love. Slow down and take in the moment. The more you practise this, the more natural it will become.

In this book, as well as recipes, you will find a collection of essays on our family rituals, born of kin and home cooking. From Eva's ritual of eating slow breakfasts on holidays (page 69) to Maria's ritual of making lasagne on her daughter's birthday (page 151) to the many rituals we observe at Christmas time (see the chapter on Advent & Christmas). Our hope is that in reading them, you will be inspired to rediscover and bring more ritual into your life and the lives of your kin. Our hope is that, like in our family, ritual becomes a deeply nourishing and connective force in your days.

How We Spice

There are some general 'rules' – much better thought of as guidelines – to using spices in your cooking. These will help as you start to build more spices into your repertoire. Importantly, we don't want you to get too caught up in the detail when approaching these. They are guidelines only, shared here with you to give you some goal posts between which you might like to shoot. They are what we have learnt over the years about how to use spices.

Storage & Selection

There are a few simple guidelines when it comes to storing and keeping spices, though the most common mistake is simply keeping them past their prime. Our grandmother had beautiful crockery and crystal glassware that were ornamentally displayed in the cupboard and rarely got used, the occasion never being quite special enough. Like her crockery, waiting for a special occasion, spices tend to sit unused in the pantry, often well past their use-by date. While old spices won't make you sick, their flavour profile will be lacking and dull, adding little to a dish. So, our number one tip is: if spices are older than a year, toss them out. The exception to this is whole spices, which last much longer than ground spices – around 5 years. Dried herbs are still pungent for up to 2 years if stored correctly. The easiest way to maintain the quality of your spices, then, is to buy high-quality spices in small quantities from a reputable source – who grinds them freshly in Australia – and to use them more frequently.

There are some other tips to help you keep your spices pungent and fresh for as long as possible. Store them:

· out of sunlight, either in a cupboard, drawer or in a tinted or opaque jar

· in an airtight jar or container – ideally glassware, not plastic

· away from moisture and condensation – keep your jars away from the stove and use a spoon to decant the spices into the pot, so steam and vapours don't enter the jar

· out of the heat, although the fridge and freezer are not recommended either.

It's worth noting that reputable sources will not use anti-caking agents or fillers to prevent the spices from clumping. Many spices are hygroscopic, which means they draw moisture from the air and therefore may clump up a little. If this occurs, simply break up the spices with the back of a spoon.

Using Spices to Elevate

When considering spices, people generally think of Indian and exotic cuisines, or spiciness in the form of chilli. While we do cook many curries and use chilli to add heat to dishes, our way of cooking with spices is less well understood. Put simply, we add spices to elevate a dish. We cook and bake the foods we love, the foods of our heritage, the foods our tastebuds desire, but we experiment with flavour and depth using spices, taking the food to another level.

Take something simple like potatoes, roasted with salt and olive oil – crunchy and absolutely delicious. You can take this dish in so many different flavour directions with spices. Add crushed coriander seeds, or a garlic and parsley combo, or a lemon myrtle, caraway seed and smoked paprika mix, and the roast potatoes instantly become more interesting and layered with so much more flavour, with very little effort. We have found inspiration – adventure, even – in cooking with spices.

Perhaps one of the best things about using spices to elevate a dish you already love, is that you're not trying a new recipe from scratch, made up of many different spices with different properties, nor are you forced to adopt a cuisine you might not be experienced with, so the chances of success are much higher. By approaching spices our way, you will familiarise yourself with their flavours, textures and properties, as you see how they transform and elevate your favourite dishes, and hopefully your cooking will grow in creativity and confidence.

How to Add Spices

Many cooks are scared of using spices. That's the reality. Even in commercial kitchens, some trained chefs are unsure of the combinations or volume of spice to use to balance a dish. Having cooked and baked with spices for almost 15 years now, we can both confidently say that this fear is unnecessary. And the secret to using spices lies in practice, experimentation and trusting your instincts.

Like any new ingredient you come across, you need to interact with a spice to become familiar with it. Smell it, taste it, read about it (the glossary and charts later in this chapter are a good starting point), discuss it with a friend or spice merchant. Be curious.

Of all these suggestions, using your nose might be the most powerful, especially if you close your eyes – switching off the distraction of sight – and deeply inhale what's before you. Humans are, we believe, born to understand food. It's imperative to our survival and, more than that, it's imperative to our wellbeing. Food does so much more than feed the body. It has the ability to nourish our whole being. And so the sense of smell helps us instinctively to categorise, weed out and connect with what is before us. If you carried out a blindfolded random smell-test of different spices, you would be surprised at exactly how much you can smell in each jar. Pick the jar that sparks the most interest in you and start experimenting with it. Try adding it in small quantities to something that you cook regularly that feels like it could benefit from the spice you have chosen. Keep tasting it as you cook. Every time you do this, you are building your knowledge bank and becoming more and more adept at using the spice.

Waking up Flavours & Aromas

Spices gain much of their flavour from the volatile oils locked in during the drying process. When this oil is released, the flavours and aromas are also released. There are various ways to achieve this, the most common being by grinding whole spices. Just after grinding, spices are most flavoursome but, over time, the flavour diminishes. There are other ways to release these oils: by crushing the spices, roasting them, or slow-cooking them whole. It is worth noting that grinding and crushing do not change the flavour profile. However, roasting intensifies the flavours, adding depth and robustness. If you plan on roasting your spices, it is best done in a frying pan without oil over high heat, making sure to keep the spices moving so they don't burn. Roasted spices do not keep very well, so only roast what you need.

Spice Blends

Even though we have been cooking with spices for a long time and are comfortable with using single spices, we have a lot of spice blends in our pantries. The ease and speed of use are big drawcards, but we also use them because, with a little time, a blend of spices melds together to create a more fully formed flavour profile than just adding individual spices as you go. Further, someone has already been through the experimentation to work out the perfect balance of spices to make a spice blend, as we do at Gewürzhaus. Spice blends are also a great starting point for anyone wanting to incorporate more spices into their everyday cooking to elevate their dishes into midweek marvels and weekend wonders. The Spice Shortcuts throughout the recipes in this book help you to determine which pre-made blends you could swap out the single spices for, should you like to incorporate spices in this way.

Fresh vs Dried Herbs

The main difference between fresh and dried herbs is the concentration of their essential oils – dried herbs have more concentrated essential oils, fresh herbs have less. Also, fresh is not always best, even though that is commonly thought the case. The important thing to consider is whether you want the fragrant top notes of a fresh herb in your dish, rather than the deeper, more robust flavours of a dried herb. You would never make tabbouleh with dried parsley as the flavour and texture would not work; on the flip side, you would never make a spaghetti sauce without using dried herbs such as oregano. Typically, when cooking, dried herbs are added towards the start of the cooking process and fresh herbs are added towards the end, or to garnish.

A Note on Salting

Salt is an essential ingredient in the kitchen. We use it alongside herbs and spices to elevate our cooking and baking. More than anything else, salt brings out the flavour in food. It helps to amalgamate and balance a dish, to highlight the flavours that might, without salt, remain hidden and less pronounced. Salt has other functions, too. Fermentation is often controlled with salt (like in Sauerkraut with Caraway, page 44) and preservation of food is done with vinegar, sugar or salt. Vegetables can become more easily digestible after a treatment with salt.

Our bodies need a certain amount of salt – sodium chloride – as it plays a key role in the functioning of our muscles and nerves and regulates water in our bodies. We don't manufacture sodium chloride in the body, so we must absorb it through our diets.

Salts vary by region, flavour and crystal structure. On one end of the scale, there's something as basic as a manufactured table salt, which gives maximum saltiness but little else. On the other end, you might find a carefully harvested sea salt crystal smoked over applewood chips, or a fine sea salt infused with black truffles. Then there are the mined salts from the Himalayas – which we reach for often in our cooking – laid down some 600,000 years ago. These are arguably the purest salts and contain the highest levels of trace elements.

Knowing when to reach for which type of salt is exceedingly useful. Crystal structure is generally the first consideration in deciding which category of salt to reach for – sea salt flakes, kosher salt or rock salt.

SEA SALT FLAKES

The relatively thin, pyramid structures of sea salt flakes, formed when sea or lake water solar-evaporates, are wonderful used as finishing salts or in dishes where you want the salt to give a pronounced salt hit while you eat. They often contain a patina of their place of origin – sea or lake – and provide a good saltiness due to the high surface area to volume ratios of their crystals. Here are our favourites to reach for.

Fleur de Sel de Guerande – a relatively wet sea salt, this is harvested off the French coast and is particularly adept at maintaining its structural integrity when served on moist or steamed foods, which allows the satisfying crunch to remain when drier salts would otherwise melt.

Pyramid flake salt – this is what we use when we call for sea salt flakes in our recipes. Originating in Pyramid Hill in western Victoria, this salt is made by pumping saline groundwater out of the Murray-Darling Basin and solar-evaporating it to produce a stronger tasting, more robust flake than the well-known pink Murray River salt. It's a great blending salt and carries the flavours of the spices and herbs very well in flavoured salts.

KOSHER SALT

This salt is designed to help in the koshering process, drawing blood from the surface of meat. Therefore, its crystals are made flatter and larger than ordinary table or sea salt, so that its surface area is maximised for the extraction process. Kosher salt also works well with fried foods, where it sticks to foods satisfyingly well.

ROCK SALT

This has a chunky and dense cell structure, so unless it is ground down to a powder or small grain, it's not useful as a finishing salt. Rather, put it in the salt pig next to your stove and use to flavour anything liquid you are cooking – soups, stews, salted water for boiling. We use fine Himalayan pink salt in many recipes, as its size allows it to break down quickly and evenly.

FLAVOURED SALTS

These tabletop gems, made of flake salt, herbs and spices, are pots of gold for sprinkling on top of a finished dish. Having had time to amalgamate their flavours with the help of the salt, which breaks down some of the molecules especially in ground spices, the resulting seasoning is moreishly good. Our Gewürzhaus favourites are Chilli Salt, Ginger & Garlic Salt, Roast Vegetable Salt and Australian Chicken Salt.

Mix & Match: Which Spices Go With Which Foods?

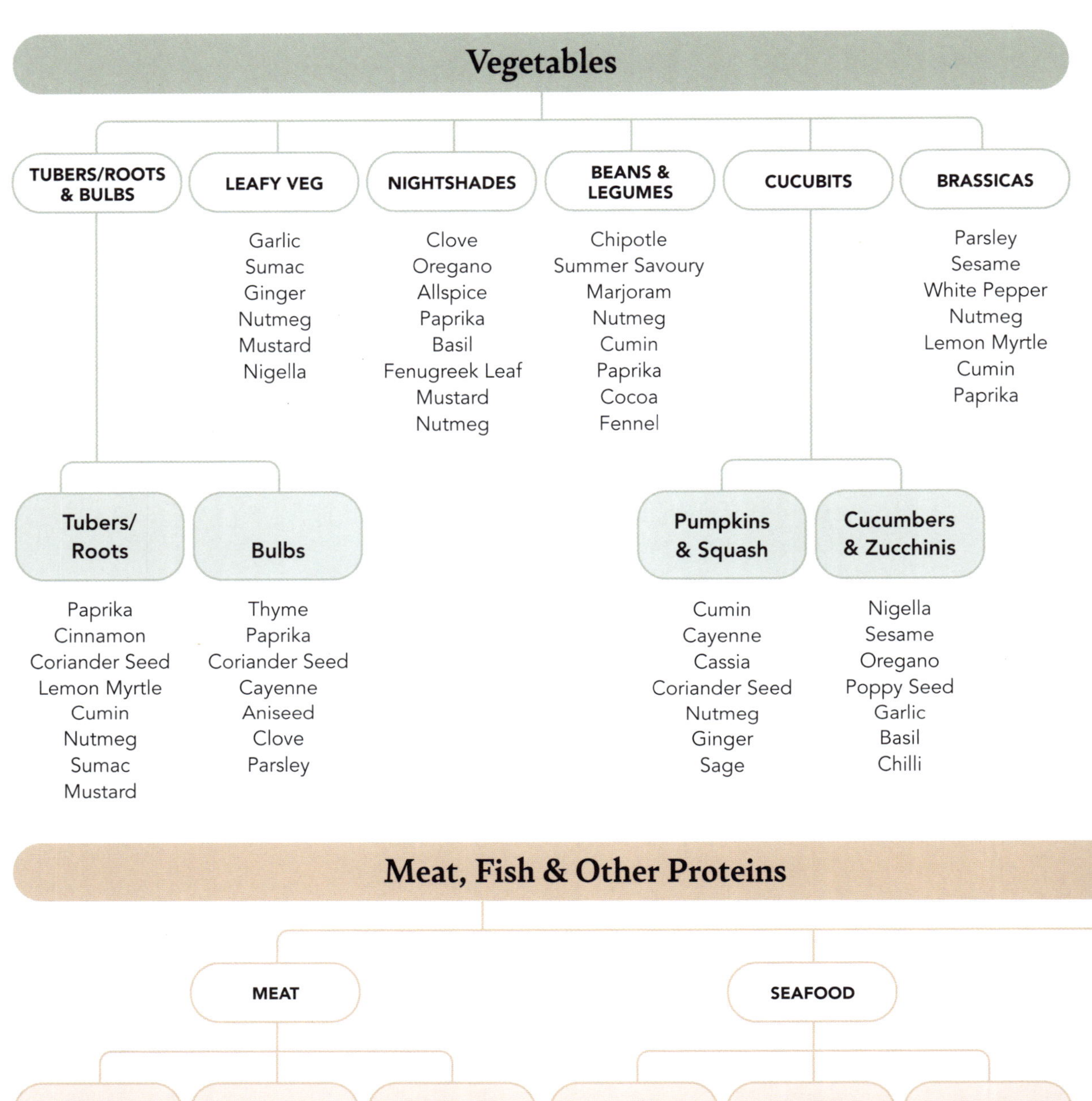

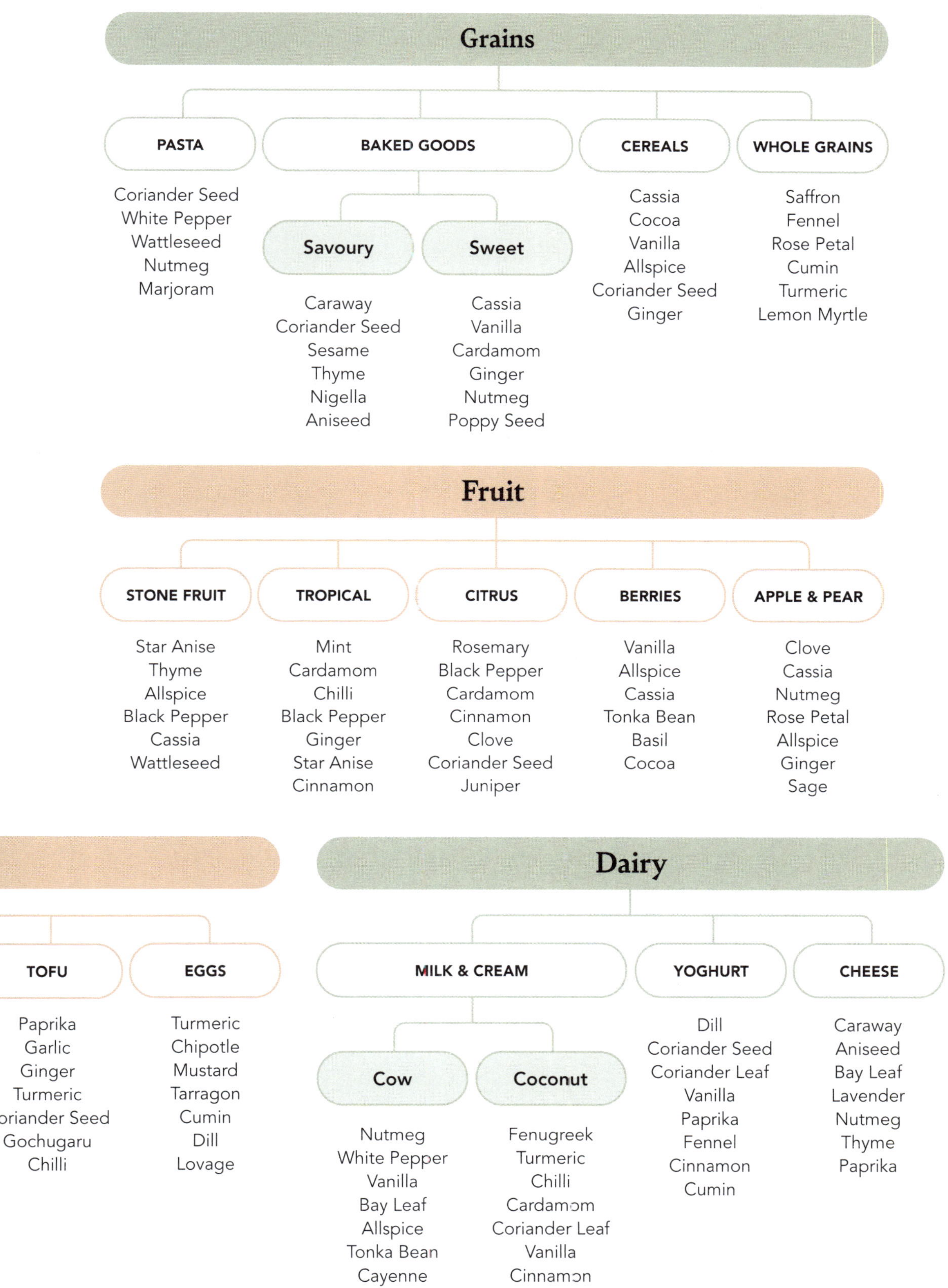

** PICK JUST ONE OR TWO OF THE SUGGESTED SPICES WHEN COOKING WITH EACH OF THESE INGREDIENTS*

Top Spices

This wheel is an easy reference for you to consider which spices you might add to your pantry to be able to cook and bake your way across most recipes in this book – adding perhaps some interesting, more unusual spices as you go.

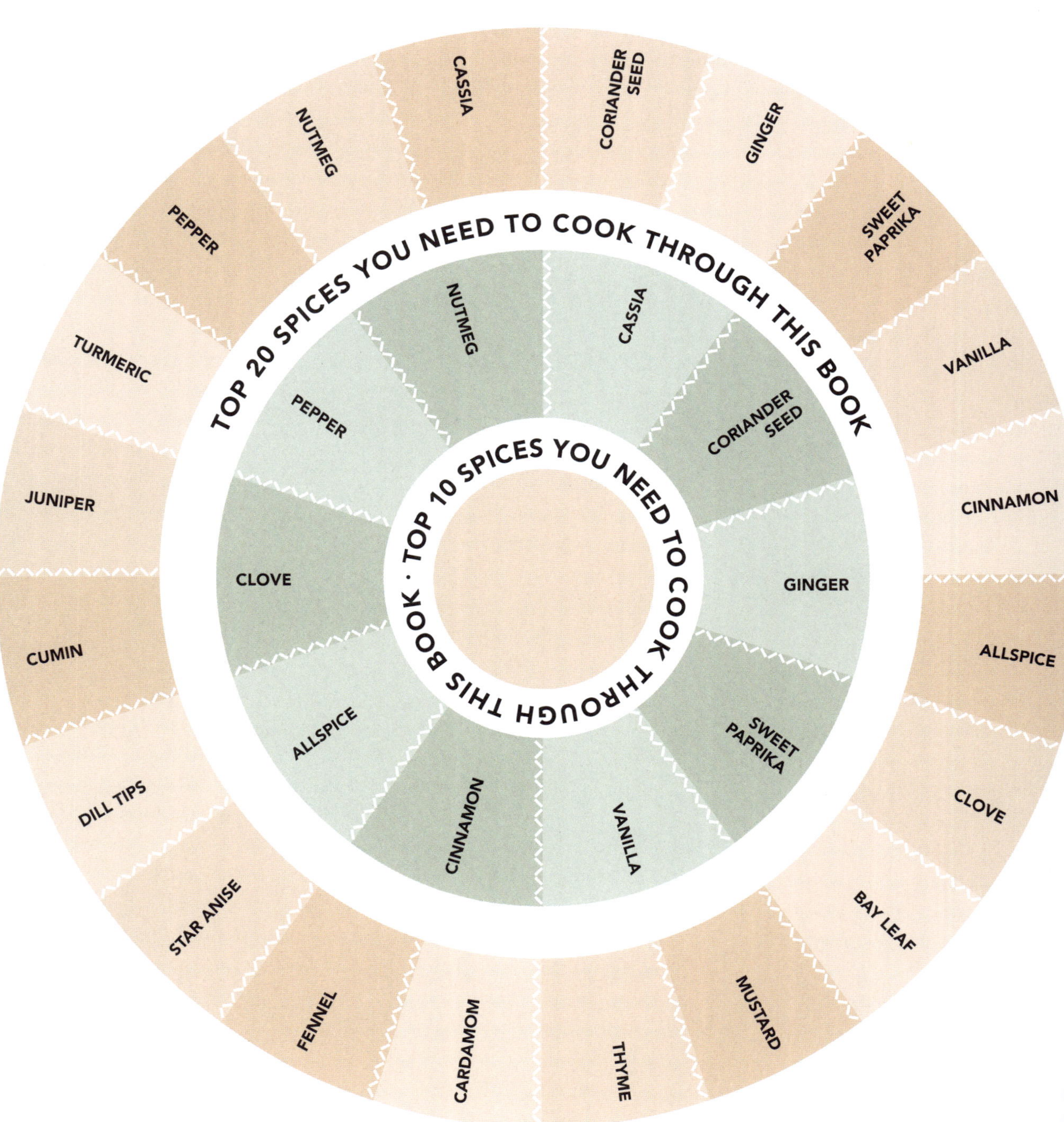

How Much Do I Use?

This chart will help you to decide how much of a spice might be appropriate to add to your dish. The spices here are categorised into how much we generally use a spice in the style of our cooking. The idea is for the spice or herb not to overpower or dominate your dish, but rather to blend in harmoniously and be balanced. If you want a dominant flavour, add more than suggested here. Star anise, for example, is in category 2, suggesting you add ¼ teaspoon of ground or equivalent whole star anise to any average-sized dish or baked good. This will keep the star anise flavour balanced with the other ingredients. If you want a dominant star anise flavour, however, you could move this to a category 3 or 4 and spice accordingly.

⅛ TSP

- BAY LEAF
- CAYENNE
- CLOVE
- LAVENDER
- PEPPERBERRY
- ROSE PETAL
- SAFFRON

¼ TSP

- ANISEED
- BASIL
- CARDAMOM
- CELERY SEED
- CHIPOTLE
- DILL TIPS
- FENUGREEK LEAF
- JUNIPER
- MACE
- PEPPER
- ROSEMARY
- STAR ANISE
- TONKA BEAN
- WATTLESEED

½ TSP

- ALLSPICE
- KASHMIRI CHILLI
- LOVAGE
- MUSTARD
- NIGELLA
- NUTMEG
- OREGANO
- PARSLEY
- SMOKED PAPRIKA
- SUMMER SAVOURY
- TARRAGON
- THYME

1 TSP

- ALEPPO PEPPER
- BLACK LIME
- CARAWAY
- CASSIA
- CHIVES
- CINNAMON
- CUMIN
- FENNEL
- GARLIC
- GINGER
- GOCHUGARU CHILLI
- MARJORAM
- VANILLA

1 TBSP

- COCOA
- CORIANDER SEED
- POPPY
- SESAME
- SWEET PAPRIKA
- TURMERIC

** FOR SPICES, THESE ARE DRIED AND GROUND*

An Unconventional Glossary of Our Favourite Spices

Although by no means extensive, the following is a glossary of the spices we most love to cook with and that are frequently included in this book. Of the 57 different herbs and spices we've used, 14 are highlighted here. There are three categories: the unsung heroes, potent and powerful, and the magic makers. Unsung heroes are those spices that work away in the background, building and enhancing, with little promise of acknowledgement when their work is done. The potent and powerful category packs a big punch and loves the headlines. They want to stand out, and will do so if you use them liberally; but, if you hold them back, they will still work their charms in the background. Lastly, the magic makers. These spices work in mysterious ways; their uncooked aromas and flavours often completely transform when exposed to heat. They have a knack for bringing flavours together to create a wonderful meal.

The Unsung Heroes

CORIANDER SEEDS

Coriander seeds get a bad rap. For years, they have been used by food manufacturers to pad out seasonings, salt blends and other dry mixes, as the seeds are readily grown and relatively cheap to buy. Often months old and devoid of their essential oils, it's not surprising you might be unimpressed when seeing them in the ingredient list of a supermarket spice blend.

However, recently harvested and freshly crushed coriander seeds will completely blow your socks off. Their essential oils are citrusy and fragrant and, once roasted, the seeds impart the most delicious and unique savoury, nutty flavour. Added to blends, their distinct flavour profile rounds out and brings together the more potent spices; in fact, coriander seeds may just be that secret ingredient you are missing. They pair equally well with sweet spices like nutmeg and cassia, and savoury ones like sage and cumin.

Coriander seeds are used in many different cuisines and are readily found in everything from curries to preserves to cakes. In this book, they're the fourth-most used spice: you'll find them in recipes like Cabbage Salad with Coriander & Caraway Oil (page 108), German Curry Ketchup (page 38) and Pistachio & Chocolate Gingerbread (page 181).

All in all, coriander seeds are one of the most important spices to use and master, and they will delight you at every turn.

NUTMEG

You might be as surprised – as we were – to find that nutmeg, after pepper, was the single most used spice in this book. We reached for it time and again in almost every chapter. Once you familiarise yourself with its complex profile, you will be adding it to everything from soups and stews to cheesecake. Nutmeg is remarkably versatile in both sweet and savoury dishes and, when whole, holds its potency for a long time – both good reasons to always have it in your pantry. It is best when freshly ground as it then releases the natural oils that make it so special.

The nutmeg we sell at Gewürzhaus is from the Banda Islands, where the spice originated from. It is sometimes referred to as Banda nutmeg and is of the highest quality. Nutmeg has long been traded on the spice markets and has quite a sad history, with many wars fought to gain control of the supply of this spice. The Banda Islands in Indonesia were first discovered by Europeans (the Portuguese) in the early 1500s. Because of the value of nutmeg and the monopoly the Portuguese had, the Dutch invaded the islands in the early 1600s and conquered the Bandanese, almost wiping out the entire population. Later, Britain temporarily took control of the islands before trading them back to the Dutch for the island of Manhattan, which then belonged to New Amsterdam.

Nutmeg is both sweet and camphorous and adds a nuttiness and depth of flavour to dishes. It pairs incredibly well with creamy dishes – just think of the smell when you grind it into your béchamel. Being both suited to sweet and savoury recipes, it works well with other spices like cinnamon, allspice, cloves, coriander and cumin as well as many more. So, make sure you keep a small jar of whole nutmeg in your pantry and freshly grate only what you need on a fine grater.

PAPRIKA

When we think about paprika, many of us associate it with Spain. However, like all *Capsicum annuum* species, the spice originated in northern South America. It was introduced to Europe through the explorer Christopher Columbus and first cultivated in Spain. This paprika, called *pimentón*, was hot in flavour with a profile similar to pepper. Much of the paprika used today, though, stems from Hungarian paprika, which has a much softer and sweeter flavour. Paprika is the national spice of Hungary and the birthplace of its name. Paprika features heavily in many of our family recipes, as the part of Romania where our grandmother grew up was previously under Hungarian rule. Despite the shifting country borders, the food culture had a lasting impact and is deeply rooted in the regions; paprika moved with the people and remains a mainstay of their cuisine. Hungarian noble sweet paprika is the overarching flavour in our Oma Rosa's Gulasch (page 98) and highlights the sweet yet pungent taste of ripe peppers, without any heat. Its crimson colour beautifully coats the meat.

Both Spanish and Hungarian paprikas come in three distinct varieties: sweet, hot and smoked.

Sweet paprika can be used generously, as it is not polarising or overpowering, and can easily be paired with other spices. Try combining it with cumin, garlic and dried herbs, such as bay leaves or rosemary. Smoked paprika is generally used more sparingly, but is a wonderful spice to add a meaty, bacon flavour to vegan and vegetarian dishes.

Paprika is a great spice that is forgiving when experimented with, and a perfect starting point for getting creative with spicing.

Potent & Powerful

BAY LEAVES

If you're going to grow just one herb-or-spice-yielding plant in your garden, a bay tree might just be the one. This might seem controversial – what about thyme? Fennel? Ginger? Basil? All worthy candidates. Yet we posit that if you have ever picked a fresh bay leaf from a tree, scrunched it up, closed your eyes and inhaled its aromas, you will understand why. The contrast between a leaf picked from your own tree and put straight into your saucepan, versus a dried leaf from a dusty supermarket shelf, is remarkable. Bay is super easy to grow at home. It is a non-fussy plant that will grow in a pot or as a hedge. If you want to pick leaves for drying, do so after a spell of hot weather, as the leaves' moisture content will be low and they will dry more quickly and flatter than when they are inflated with rainwater.

The profile of bay leaves changes significantly when dried, as with many herbs – the fresh leaf is super potent, almost overpowering, and bitter if overused. The dried leaf is more mellow and balanced, yet lacks the *je ne sais quoi* of the just-released essential oils of a freshly picked leaf. Where you might comfortably add two or three dried bay leaves to a dish, even one fresh leaf might be too much.

Bay leaf, both dried and fresh, is camphorous, peppery and grassy-sweet. It imparts a distinct, lingering and uplifting taste and aroma to many dishes, such as soups and stews, rich and fatty casseroles, béchamel and dairy-based sauces, and preserves. It likes the company of other big and bold ingredients: spices like nutmeg, cloves and juniper, vegetables like tomatoes and eggplant, and meats like pork belly and oxtail.

CARAWAY SEEDS

Caraway has a long history in our family. Grown all across mainland Europe, it has been used by generations of women in our line to season preserves, bread, meat and other specialties. Caraway, like dill, is an acquired taste that took both of us time to appreciate. As kids, our youthful palates were not keen on the flavour. For Maria, it was actually a rye and caraway bread from Aldi that she started buying in her university days that won her over. The marriage of caraway seeds with milled grains is a long, enduring one – steady and familiar, unique yet not showy. The gluten-free buckwheat and brown rice sourdough that Maria now bakes is never without a few heaped tablespoons of these ancient and hardworking seeds.

Shake up a jar of caraway seeds and the aromas will hit you with their potency. Savoury and bread like, with a hint of anise, you can see how this spice pairs well with rich and fatty meats, particularly pork, where caraway's essential oils help to bring balance to a heavy dish. Grains, especially rye and buckwheat, are classic caraway combinations and enhance their flavour profiles, but equally, a puffy and freshly baked crescent (page 224) is enhanced by a sprinkling of caraway and good-quality salt, baked on with a lick of egg wash. Sauerkraut (page 44) is often speckled with caraway seeds, and for good reason, as cabbage and caraway are great partners. Stewed or baked apples, cheese and seeded crackers all get a lift from caraway, too.

If you haven't yet cooked with this delicious spice, please do. Although it takes some getting used to, once you master it, your food will be better for it.

CLOVES

Cloves are one of the most widely utilised spices in our homes. We have two jars of whole cloves and a jar of ground in the kitchen, plus a mini tin of whole cloves in our medical travel kit.

Cloves make a wonderful addition to many dishes. Pungent and sweet, warm and medicinal, strongly flavoured and so delightfully complex, smelling a jar of cloves makes us think of sweet and sticky apricots, semi dried in the hot summer sun, coupled with a hint of camphor. Their deeply layered flavours best unfold when you infuse your food with the whole buds. Cloves have a place in many different cuisines and dishes – from marmalades to marble cake, fish pie to red cabbage – but one of our favourite ways to showcase this spice is in preserves. Green tomato pickles are lost without cloves, and they are the secret ingredient in most good ketchups, adding not only complexity but also sweetness. Of course, Christmas fare is studded (sorry!) with cloves right across the different courses: Christmas-Spiced Roast Duck (page 250), Spekulaas Spiced Cookies (page 235) and Winter Warming Mulled Wine (page 272) all draw on cloves for their flavours. Around the world, cloves are used in curries and stews, to flavour grains and vegetables, and in stewing fruits (apples and pears are particularly delicious with cloves).

As to why cloves feature in our medical kit, they are a potent antiseptic and have been used in dentistry since ancient times. The active ingredient in cloves is an oil called eugenol. It's a mild anaesthetic particularly good for the gums, teeth and mouth tissue. Brewing up half a dozen whole cloves in hot water and leaving them to steep overnight makes a great natural mouthwash, which can also be gargled throughout the day to help keep a sore throat at bay. We use it in place of pharmaceutical gargles and lozenges. After rinsing, don't spit out the liquid as the clove water will help you fight infection in the rest of your system, too.

The next time you pull a clove bud out of its jar, you will have myriad ideas on how to use it. Further, consider that this humble spice singlehandedly paid for Magellan's first circumnavigation of the world in 1522 – 381 sacks of Moluccan clove, to be exact. They outlasted the captain and most of his crew, and still grace our kitchens today, making the long journey from their fragrant trees across the shores to our spice jars.

DILL TIPS

Dill is a notable herb in European cultures, especially in Eastern European and Scandinavian countries. It is delicate and aromatic, with a sweet flavour and an undertone of anise. It is mostly used in savoury dishes where its distinct flavour is quite prominent. Almost every pickle recipe will call for dill tips (the green tips of the leaves) with the grassy freshness complementing sour flavours so well. It is the star ingredient in Eva's beloved childhood dish, Eggs with Mustard & Dill Sauce (page 115). We also use it in salad dressings, sauces and soups. It has so much flavour that it is great as a hero ingredient. However, the herb also pairs well with other soft herbs and spices, such as mustard seeds, garlic and turmeric.

This is one of our favourite herbs for the freshness it adds.

PEPPERCORNS

Pepper, along with salt, has made it to the centre of most kitchen tables. That's quite a feat. Yet we take pepper for granted, adding it to food automatically and without much thought. Pepper, though, is capable of so much.

For one, there are several types of true pepper (*Piper nigrum*) that are readily available to buy: black, white and green peppercorns. All from the same plant, this trio is differentiated by how they are processed once off the vine, yielding distinct flavour profiles.

Green pepper is the fruitiest and gentlest, its heat hitting the palate much later than black and white pepper. It can be used more liberally and pairs particularly well with sweet custardy desserts, salads and creamy, ripe fruit like pears. Black pepper is the most aromatic and flavourful of the three, its pericarp (outer skin) containing the pungent oil, piperine. Freshly ground black pepper breathes life into anything it touches – steak, sautéed asparagus, a hard-boiled egg, a slice of buttered fruit toast. It accentuates any food with its complex and unfolding symphony of heat, flavour and potent essential oils. Use it more sparingly than the other two peppers, as it can overpower other spices and flavours. White pepper is less complex than the other two, having had the outer pericarp removed. It provides an even heat and toned-down black-pepper flavour that makes it an excellent choice in white sauces, pâté and savoury baked goods. It's an important component of the spice blend quatre épices, one of our favourite seasonings to reach for in autumn and winter.

A mix of the three peppercorns makes a great blend for pepper grinders.

The Magic Makers

ALLSPICE

If Italy is basil, the Caribbean Islands must be allspice. There's sugar and spice and all things nice – things all found in the little, round berry we call allspice. Perhaps more than any other spice, allspice really is everything. Warming and sweet, yet at the same time peppery and medicinal, the aroma of allspice is that of a generously spiced rum. It has the depth of maple syrup, the sharpness of black peppercorns and the medicinal characteristics of basil or bay leaf.

Like cloves, allspice contains the essential oil eugenol, and there is significant similarity between the two spices. Allspice, though, is less overpowering than cloves. It mellows and blends when cooked or baked. If cloves have a tendency to fight and dominate, allspice is relaxed and friendly.

Allspice is the seventh-most used spice in this book – proof of its versatility and charm. You'll find it in baked goods, partnered with the usual sweet suspects cassia, cinnamon and cloves, but also with wattleseed and cocoa. It is magical with ground nuts, particularly almond and hazelnut, and delightful with stone fruit like plums and cherries. Chicken liver pâté and other charcuterie like ham is better off with the addition of allspice. A sauce of sweet, salty and acidic elements can be improved with allspice – add a little and it will work away in the background to bring the flavours together, or add a lot to make it the hero. Meats like duck and pork, and game like venison, are delicious with allspice, particularly combined with juniper berry and bay leaves. Vegetables, such as sweet potato and tomato, as well as veg or fish curries often include allspice for the breadth of flavour it adds.

CASSIA VS CINNAMON

Like hotel vs motel, motorway vs freeway, straw vs hay, they are all same same but different. Cassia and cinnamon are in this category and deserve differentiating when it comes to their culinary uses.

Cassia is the outer bark of the *Cinammomum cassia* tree, while cinnamon is the rolled inner bark of the *Cinnamomum verum* tree. Cassia is more pungent and darker in colour. Cinnamon is sweet with delicate top notes, and lighter in colour than cassia.

In many countries, Australia included, much of the cinnamon or cinnamon-flavoured foods you buy are actually made with cassia, especially baked goods like cinnamon scrolls, which are really cassia scrolls. This does not make cassia inferior to cinnamon, or vice versa; they are just a little different, and it is worth understanding their uniqueness.

As a general rule, it's good to think about how dominant you would like the 'cinnamon flavour' to be. Cinnamon is much more subtle, delicate and refined, often the choice for curries, savoury dishes and pared-back sweets. Cassia packs more of a punch and stands up to heat somewhat better than true cinnamon.

SAFFRON

Saffron is one of our favourite spices. That's a huge call with so many delicious spices to choose from. However, it is the depth of flavour and beautiful colour that saffron adds to a dish that wins us over. It is earthy, sweet and slightly bitter, with floral and almost toasted caramel or honey notes. Saffron has a distinct undertone that just elevates what you have cooked to the next level.

There are a few handy tips that will help you get the most out of saffron. Ideally, steep the stigmas (threads) in a little hot water for at least 30 minutes before using the liquid with the stigmas in your dish. This way, the flavour is released and you get the best out of the world's most expensive spice. Secondly, use it quite sparingly. A small pinch – think 10–20 stigmas – goes a long way and, like lavender, if you use too much it can be overpowering and lose its appeal. It pairs well with cinnamon, vanilla, cumin, coriander and nutmeg, and it is also a key ingredient in the complex Moroccan spice blend ras el hanout, which often contains more than 20 ingredients.

Similar to vanilla, saffron is very labour intensive to produce. Saffron is the stigma plucked from the purple-flowered crocus. Each bloom has only three stigmas, and a 2-hectare plot yields between 500 and 750 grams of this handpicked spice. The crocus flower opens its leaves at sunrise and whenever we are cooking with saffron, the colour reminds us of this.

STAR ANISE

Star anise would have to be one of our favourite spices, if not our absolute favourite. It is often misunderstood as being exclusively a spice for Asian dishes, but it has so much more to offer. Sweet, liquorice like and medicinal, to us, star anise is life. It is full of contrasts and oomph, showing up in big and bold ways. When it finds the right partners, it gives generously and enhances flavours and aromas.

Our hands-down favourite application of star anise is with plums. When stewed with star anise, they are hard to beat, especially when doused in a swig of good rum (page 262), another of star anise's friends. A hot toddy with a couple of star anise, a few cloves, half a lemon and some maple syrup to sweeten is our go-to winter warming night-time drink. All stone fruit is great with this spice, as is Christmas baking and cooking. On the savoury side, beef, pork and smoked meats are enhanced by star anise, as are hearty soups and stews.

THYME

The versatility of thyme reaches far wider than its culinary appeal – for centuries, it has also been used as incense and for medicinal purposes. In many European cultures, it is believed that *Schnaps* helps to cure ailments and to fight viruses and we too have included thyme in our recipe for Cherry & Thyme Liqueur (page 274). Here, the infusion creates an essential oil–filled cure for adults to swig at bedtime to help fight off a cough or cold. Its antibacterial properties also make it a much-used ingredient for natural cough remedies, and many ailment-specific teas will include thyme.

In culinary terms, thyme is widely used, being a key ingredient in many spice blends for flavouring meat, vegetables, stews and soups. We have used it in many recipes throughout this book, often as a feature, but also to support other flavour profiles. Paired with ginger, lavender or lemon myrtle, thyme is also a great addition to sweet treats. In savoury dishes, it is a pretty perfect match with nutmeg, but also many other spices, such as paprika and coriander.

VANILLA

The beauty of vanilla begins at its place of origin, Mexico, a country so rich in colour and flavour and deep history. Vanilla shares much of the enchantment of its homeland. The vanilla plant is a climbing orchid, which clings to a host tree with hanging roots. The pods, or beans, are formed after the orchid has bloomed and then the magical transformation work starts with processing the fresh pod – which has almost no vanilla aroma or taste – first done by the Aztecs. Most vanilla crops are hand pollinated and it takes 6–9 months from pollination for the pods to be ready to harvest. The pods are then dried out in a kiln for 24 hours, turning the enzymes into vanillin. They are then spread out to sun-dry for a further 28 days. At the end of each day, the pods are gathered and wrapped in blankets or straw mats to sweat overnight. They may then be stored up to another 6 months until finally cured. During this process, 5 kilograms of fresh vanilla ends up as 1 kilogram of cured vanilla and each pod has been handled up to 100 times.

Vanilla works in mysterious ways. Sometimes, when a cake just doesn't taste right, vanilla will fix it. Its aroma is generally fragrant, floral and sweet. However, depending on what it is prepared with, how it is used and what the origin of the pod is, the flavour can develop quite differently, although equally deliciously. When the pod is split open, the tiny seeds are scraped out and used in a variety of desserts. You can place the used pod into your sugar jar and infuse the sugar to make vanilla sugar. Alternatively, if you are stewing or poaching, add the split pod to the cooking process for extra flavour, then later discard. Vanilla partners well with other sweet spices, such as cinnamon and cassia, and helps to balance more pungent spices like star anise and cloves.

Despite being more expensive, it's worth buying quality plump and glossy pods or true extract over imitation vanilla.

Cook's Notes

Everyone has their own ways in the kitchen. Ours are laid out here to help you navigate the recipes that follow. We particularly encourage you to reduce consumables in the kitchen, and to compost your scraps if possible.

Equipment & Techniques

Teaspoons and tablespoons: In Australia, 4 teaspoons are equal to 1 tablespoon or 20 ml, not to be confused with American measures, where 3 teaspoons equate to 1 tablespoon or 15 ml. It is worth checking your measuring utensils as many come from the USA.

Spice shortcuts: For many recipes, we have provided shortcuts to using Gewürzhaus spice blends. In the ingredients lists, we have placed an asterisk after the spices that you can replace with the given quantity of a Gewürzhaus blend.

Sterilising glass jars: Our preferred way to sterilise clean jars and glass lids is in the oven. Place them in a cold oven and bake them for 20 minutes at 130°C. If your oven is old and slow to heat, add another 10 minutes to this time. Ideally, do this the day before you begin as the jars need to be cool before filling. Sterilise metal lids and rubber seals in a saucepan of water with a dash of white vinegar on medium heat for a few minutes.

Heat-treating: We prefer to heat-treat via a water bath canning system. Fill your sterilised jars with whatever you wish to preserve. Work with clean and sterile utensils. Generally, don't fill right to the top – leave a two-finger gap, especially with liquid-containing preserves. Seal your jars, place into your canning machine and cover with water that is a similar temperature to your preserves. Now heat-treat the jars according to the recipe instructions. Note that the timings given are from when the water bath reaches the desired temperature, not from cold.

Pressure cooking: In Germany, a pressure cooker is almost as important to a household as a barbecue is to Australians. We use our pressure cookers often. They are probably our favourite kitchen tool: practical, super quick to cook food, fantastic for batch cooking. Also, a pressure cooker locks in the flavours of your dish and concentrates them. Meat and vegetables hold their shape and don't turn to mush. A further time-saving tip is to release the pressure after cooking by putting the pressure cooker in the kitchen sink and running cold water over the pot for a minute. If you want to invest in a pressure cooker, we recommend the brands Silit and Fissler. Buy a stainless-steel one rather than non-stick or ceramic. If you intend to bulk cook for your family, we highly recommend purchasing at least a 5 litre pressure cooker.

Mixers: We prefer handheld electric mixers as this is the tool we each have in our homes, but all of the recipes can be made with either a stand mixer or handheld electric mixer, so use what you're comfortable with.

Lining trays and pans: We try to steer clear of single-use consumables. When lining a baking tray, we use silicone baking sheets that can be washed in the washing machine or sink after each use. For cake tins, we coat the entire inside of the tin with butter and then sprinkle the greased tin with a little flour, shaking it around while rotating the tin until it is completely dusted with flour. Then tap out any excess. On occasion, if we need a perfect edge, we will use brown baking paper.

Wraps: We prefer reusable wraps, such as beeswax wraps or silicone wraps, instead of clingwrap or ziplock bags. If you do use ziplock bags, you can hand wash them and re-use.

Ingredients

Almond meal: Ideally, buy whole raw almonds and grind them in a food processor as you need them. The almond meal will be fresher this way.

Olive oil: Always extra-virgin olive oil.

Vinegar: In some recipes, we stipulate apple cider vinegar with the mother. Using an active vinegar is important, as the mother is what allows fermentation to occur. An active vinegar is also great for gut health.

Vegetables: We try to reduce waste and use whole vegetables where possible. Where a recipe calls for a vegetable, for example, a leek, we are referring to the entire vegetable, so use the green tops as well as the white.

Ethical sourcing: We encourage you to think about the source of your food. We buy and grow free range, organic, local and in season wherever possible and practical. We do this especially for eggs, meat, vegetables and sugar.

Composting: In our homes, we compost our food waste. If your council doesn't provide this service for you, invest in a worm farm, Bokashi or compost system to turn your scraps into soil.

Useful Things

'There are certain foods, like sauerkraut, that come to mind when you think of a culture or country. Foods that, if removed, would completely change the story of a nation or a people. Things like kimchi for Koreans, passata for Italians, mole for Mexicans, borscht for Ukrainians and, well, sauerkraut for Germans.'

Everything Pantry Vinaigrette

ALLES-VINAIGRETTE

Making your own all-purpose salad dressing is so easy. You can use excellent-quality oils and vinegars, rather than the so-common canola and vegetable oils used in even the more expensive store-bought dressings. I keep a jar of this in the pantry at all times. You can then throw together a salad (sometimes it's even just lettuce!) and pour over the ready-to-use dressing. The dill tips add a lovely freshness to the dressing without their distinct flavour coming through too much. – ***Maria***

MAKES 500 ML (2 CUPS)
Gluten free / Dairy free / Vegan

- 100 ml red wine vinegar
- 60 ml (3 tbsp) white wine vinegar
- 30 ml (1½ tbsp) apple cider vinegar
- 10 ml (2 tsp) gluten-free light soy sauce or gluten-free tamari
- 2 tbsp A Good Staple Mustard (page 48) or Dijon mustard
- 30 ml (1½ tbsp) maple syrup
- 1 tbsp dried red onion flakes*
- 2 tsp dried chives*
- 2 tsp dried parsley*
- ½ tsp dried dill tips*
- freshly cracked black pepper*
- 200 ml extra-virgin olive oil

SPICE SHORTCUTS*
2 tbsp Gewürzhaus Salad Herbs, Gewürzhaus Italian Herbs or Gewürzhaus Herbes de Provence

Place all the ingredients, except the oil, in a 700 ml sterilised glass jar (see page 29 for instructions). Seal the jar and shake vigorously for about 1 minute. Add the oil and shake again to combine.

Store in the pantry for several months. Shake before use.

Crunchy Chilli Oil

SCHNELLES UND LECKERES CHILLIÖL

This might just become your little hack for pimping up every meal. It is full of flavour and texture. It can be used either in cooking or as a condiment and goes incredibly well with stir-fries, scrambled eggs, noodle dishes, toasties, dumplings or anything else, really!

MAKES 800 G
Dairy free / Vegan

- 750 ml (3 cups) neutral oil (canola, vegetable or grapeseed)
- 1 French shallot, finely sliced*
- 1 tbsp crushed garlic*
- 1 tsp crushed ginger*
- 65 g (½ cup) gochugaru chilli flakes*
- 3 tbsp Aleppo pepper*
- 3 tbsp golden sesame seeds*
- 2 tsp crushed coriander seeds*
- 2 tsp coconut sugar
- 1 tsp sea salt flakes*
- 3 tbsp light soy sauce

SPICE SHORTCUTS*
200 g Gewürzhaus Crunchy Chilli Oil Blend

Heat the oil in a saucepan over medium heat, then add the shallot, garlic and ginger. Fry until golden brown, about 10 minutes. Strain and spread out the mixture on a plate to cool.

Place the strained oil back into the saucepan and heat to 180°C. It is easiest to use a candy thermometer for this. If you don't have one, try to heat the oil as hot as possible before it reaches smoking point.

In the meantime, mix all the remaining ingredients together in a heatproof bowl – ceramic is ideal. Pour the hot oil directly on the chilli mixture and stir to combine. The aroma of the oil hitting the spices is incredible! Add the shallot mixture and stir it through.

Decant the oil into a sterilised jar (see page 29 for instructions). Store in a cool, dark place, like the pantry, for up to 6 months.

COOK'S NOTES: *This blend is quite mild in heat. If you'd like your chilli oil to pack more punch, substitute the Aleppo pepper for a hotter chilli flake of your choice. Or you can keep the Aleppo and also add 3 tablespoons of a hotter chilli. Use gluten-free soy sauce to make this oil gluten free.*

CRUNCHY
CHILLI OIL
BLEND
120g
coarse

Coriander & Caraway Oil

KORIANDER-UND KÜMMELÖL

The deliciously warming smells of toasted caraway, cumin and coriander seeds will fill your home when you make this oil. Pour it over all manner of vegetables and meats: it goes particularly well with cabbage (page 108), roasted red capsicum, tomatoes and parsley-based salads. Lamb backstrap with some fresh cucumber and a big dollop of hummus topped with this oil makes a lovely, easy summer meal. You could add some lemon peel to the warm oil for a more citrusy version.

MAKES 300 ML
Gluten free / Dairy free / Vegan

- 2 tbsp coriander seeds
- 3 tsp caraway seeds
- 1 tsp cumin seeds
- 1½ tsp fine Himalayan pink salt
- 250 ml (1 cup) extra-virgin olive oil
- 1 fresh bay leaf

In a heavy-based frying pan, roast the spices over medium–low heat until aromatic and starting to brown. Pound the spices and salt using a mortar and pestle until they are well bruised and crushed, about 30 seconds.

Transfer to a small saucepan or an enamel measuring jug over low heat. Add the oil and heat slowly until the oil is very watery – don't bring it to a simmer or even smoking point, just gently heat it.

Place the bay leaf in a 400 ml sterilised bottle or jar (see page 29 for instructions), then pour the warmed oil in. Seal and store in the pantry. The flavours will develop more over time, but you can use it straight away. Keeps as long as olive oil stays fresh.

COOK'S NOTES: *If you dip your finger in this oil and taste it, it might seem quite salty. It is designed to be drizzled directly on food so you probably won't have to season again. You can reduce the salt in the oil, if you like.*

CORIANDER & CARAWAY OIL, CRUNCHY CHILLI OIL (PAGE 34)

German Curry Ketchup

GEWÜRZKETCHUP

Gewürzketchup is found at every German barbecue (yes, Germans barbecue!). It is only mildly hot, full of spices, and has a distinct sweetness owing to the addition of red capsicum, pineapple and brown sugar.

MAKES ABOUT 1.2 LITRES
Gluten free / Dairy free / Vegan

140 g sweet pineapple
1 kg beefsteak tomatoes
1 red capsicum
1 large red onion, peeled
4 garlic cloves, peeled
80 g brown sugar
50 g tomato paste
125 ml (½ cup) red wine vinegar
80 ml (⅓ cup) rice malt syrup

Spices

2 tbsp yellow mustard seeds
1 tbsp coriander seeds
1 tbsp sweet paprika
1 tbsp ground turmeric
1 tsp dried fenugreek leaf
½ tsp ground allspice
1 tsp freshly ground black pepper
1 tsp mild chilli flakes
1 tsp ground cloves
1 tsp ground cinnamon
1 tsp ground ginger
¼ tsp ground nutmeg
¼ tsp celery seeds
⅛ tsp cayenne pepper
1 tsp fine Himalayan pink salt

Remove the skin from the pineapple. Roughly chop the pineapple, tomatoes, capsicum, onion and garlic. Place in a food processor and process on high speed until you have a smooth paste, about 10–15 seconds.

Pour the mixture into a large, heavy-based saucepan and place the lid on the pan on an angle, so the steam can escape. Simmer over medium–low heat for about 35 minutes, stirring regularly. Don't let the sauce get too thick or reduce too much, as you'll end up with the consistency of tomato paste.

Add 125 ml (½ cup) of water and all the remaining ingredients and spices. Stir them in well and gently simmer for a further 20 minutes, stirring regularly.

Remove the pan from the heat and leave to cool for at least 30 minutes. Return the mixture to the food processor and process for 1 minute on high speed into a smooth sauce. Scrape down the side and lid. Process for a further minute, or until the ketchup is super smooth. Test the consistency and add a little more water if you like it runnier.

Transfer to sterilised bottles or jars (see page 29 for instructions). Heat-treat in a water bath at 100°C for 30 minutes (see page 29). Store in the pantry for up to 1 year. Once opened, store in the fridge and, if using jars, always use a clean spoon to retrieve your ketchup to prevent mould.

COOK'S NOTES: *You can use a Thermomix to make this ketchup. Process the tomatoes, capsicum, pineapple, onion and garlic for 10 sec/speed 9. Cook for 50 min/100°C/speed 2–3 with the lid off (you can cover with the Thermo basket to prevent splattering). Add the remaining ingredients and cook for a further 20 min/100°C/speed 2–3 with the lid off. Cool in place, then purée for 2 min/speed 10.*

ON SAUERKRAUT & FOOD LINES

'Our food lines hold our story. And that story, no matter what it is – whether it's pretty or ugly, whether it's grand or humble, whether our noodle is a spaghetti or a *kway tiao* – holds richness and grit and love and loss.'

When I make sauerkraut, I take my time with the process. I make sure the kids won't be home and that there is peace in the house. As I shred and shred cabbage, the morning sun shining dappled through the window, I think about the many, many generations before me who did this exact same thing, to preserve the harvest and prepare for the cold winter months. I think about the mound of cabbages that they would have processed, the shredding becoming cathartic once I find my rhythm, and I wonder whether they, too, found it so.

Sauerkraut is such an iconic food, partly, I believe, because the process of making it hasn't changed. We haven't figured out how to make better sauerkraut than our ancestors did. It comes down to the freshness and quality of the cabbage and the care and attention we give to the process, none of these things particularly aided by the technological advantages of our times. It's largely about nuance and judgement, about feeling your way through the process. That's when you have mastered it – when you know intuitively what to do and when.

Sauerkraut hasn't always been made in our family. Eva and I have only recently come to it, and neither our parents nor our grandparents made sauerkraut in our lifetimes. Yet there are stories of its making. Our mum, in her hippie young adulthood, says she made it. Further back, our great-grandparents on both sides almost certainly made it. There's a very real possibility that our paternal ancestors carried it with them in a barrel as they made the gruelling journey from Germany to the settlements in the East – to current-day Romania and the Czech Republic. On Mum's side, sauerkraut was also made to get the family through the cold northern German and Polish winters. These areas were good for growing cabbage. Sauerkraut, almost without a doubt, runs in our family, and pervasively so.

There are certain foods, like sauerkraut, that come to mind when you think of a culture or country. Foods that, if removed, would completely change the story of a nation or a people. Things like kimchi for Koreans, passata for Italians, mole for Mexicans, borscht for Ukrainians and, well, sauerkraut for Germans.

They are foods that can tell us a lot about a place and its people. What do they grow? Is their land by the sea? Are their winters long and cold? Are their summers hot and tropical? Often, there is a hero ingredient that is uniquely utilised in a certain way and has been cultivated in these lands for a long time. Sometimes, the food was born out of a famine or war, or out of a very practical need to make use of a glut of local produce. Other times, it's the method of making this food that makes it special.

Of course, it's not always as linear or orderly or alliterate as 'kimchi for Koreans'. In fact, it's hardly ever this simple when looking back over a prolonged period of time at the lines that food travels along. Borders on maps rarely contain these foods neatly within their boundaries. More often than not, these foods run along ethnic or regional lines rather than in countries, and they jump around, too: wars and hardships result in changes in borders and the movement of people, geography separates areas and so on. Trying to trace the movement of these foods on a map would be a messy business, the lines snaking everywhere, like a big plateful of entangled spaghetti.

Consider this plate of spaghetti. Imagine that each noodle represents just one person's food line. Along it, that noodle contains the foods that the person's ancestors prepared and ate, holding our 'foodprint' like a strand of DNA. I like to think about my food heritage in this way, as a food line. I like to think about being *made* in this way; that our DNA is built not just of nucleotides, but of freshly fermented cucumbers and gulasch and rye bread and chicken broth and hot morello cherries poured over countless different bowls of semolina porridge. We are made of the foods that the mother of our mother's mother made. And the mother of our father's mother. All the way there and much further back. We are built of the foods they ate to endure war and famine. And the foods they prepared when their vegetable plots were bursting at the seams with life and chlorophyl and hot, sweet fruit juices.

Our food lines hold our story. And that story, no matter what it is – whether it's pretty or ugly, whether it's grand or humble, whether our noodle is a spaghetti or a *kway tiao* – holds richness and grit and love and loss. And more than loss, it is a story of survival, because you are here, aren't you? Against many odds, you are here. Understanding that story – understanding and discovering all those wonderful and not so wonderful foods on our noodles – is immensely grounding and enriching. Because from it, you will understand that you belong here and that you have a place here, and that that has always been the way.

Discovering your food line is a journey of adventure. It's also a journey of healing. It's a worthy, lifelong pursuit. Most likely, you will engage in its discovery with different degrees of fervour at different stages of your life. It starts with eating as a child. It moves to questioning and sometimes rejecting as a teenager. It flows on to cooking some of the dishes familiar to you as a young adult. When you become a mother or father, there is an important passing of the baton that occurs, a rite of passage, as you begin feeding the next generation with the food on their food line. As you enter the next phase of your life, you might delve deeper into the foods on your food line that you haven't yet cooked or tasted. Recipes passed down yet forgotten, foods more generally of your heritage but which perhaps skipped a generation. You take the time to rediscover – because the food is already a part of you, whether you are aware of it or not – and in doing so, there is an enormous potential for healing and for reconnection. And maybe, just maybe, you will see in a flash the line of your ancestors, close and distant, each holding a plate of something they prepared and ate in their lifetimes. A line that is long and deep and colourful and immensely rich. A line that is your line.

– Maria

Sauerkraut with Caraway

SAUERKRAUT MIT KÜMMEL

Making sauerkraut is so satisfying. You take nothing more than a fresh cabbage and a seemingly small amount of salt, and you turn it into a delicious, tangy, long-lasting and highly nutritious food that can accompany anything from breakfast eggs to a ploughman's lunch to a bowl of hot Asian-style soup. Go through the steps before you start and take your time. Once you have the hang of making sauerkraut, you won't be able to walk past good-looking cabbages without acquiring them ever again. – ***Maria***

MAKES 2 × 1 LITRE JARS
Gluten free / Dairy free / Vegan

1 large, fresh cabbage, ideally organic (about 1.5 kg)

fine Himalayan pink salt

caraway seeds

For this recipe, you'll need a mandoline, kitchen scale, two 1 litre glass jars with glass lids and two glass weights (I use small glass jars). Choose vessels with a roughly even body and no narrow openings – Weck-style or Le Parfait-style jars work best. Sterilise your clean jars, lids and weights (see page 29 for instructions). Ideally, do this the day before you begin as the jars need to be cool before filling.

Start by removing any spoilt outer leaves of the cabbage and placing them in the compost. Remove two healthy leaves and cut out two round discs. These should be slightly smaller than the opening of your jars and will act as barriers to submerge the cabbage in its own liquid. Use the jar lids as your stencils. Include the thick spine of the leaf in your disc, so that the discs have enough structure to hold down the cabbage. Set them aside.

Wash the cabbage head, then quarter it through the core. Using a mandoline, finely slice each cabbage segment. Slice the remainder of the cut-out leaves. Transfer to a large bowl, weighing the cabbage. Record the weight.

Add 1.4% salt to the cabbage – so 14 g of salt for every 1 kg of cabbage. The more salt you add, the slower your cabbage will ferment, though much more than 1.4% and you will end up with very salty sauerkraut.

Next, toss the salt through the cabbage thoroughly. Don't massage or work the cabbage. This method will yield a crunchier sauerkraut. If you prefer a softer sauerkraut, toss the salt through, then massage the cabbage. Set aside for 20 minutes. The cabbage will have reduced in volume and should be dripping liquid when you pick some up out of the bowl.

CONTINUED OVERLEAF >

Add about 1 teaspoon of caraway seeds per 1 kg of cabbage and toss it through the cabbage.

Next, transfer your cabbage into the sterilised jars. Start by weighing the empty jar and record the weight. Add a handful of cabbage at a time, pressing down firmly about 20 times between each layer to remove any air bubbles and release juices to backfill the space. Sauerkraut requires an oxygen-free environment to ferment successfully. If there are air bubbles in your kraut, your ferment could go soft, change colour, or develop mould or yeast.

For the jar configuration I use, I add 770 g of cabbage to the jar. That leaves enough space to still add the cabbage leaf and then the weight on top, followed by the jar lid. You will need to play around with this. Find a standard jar and weight that work for you and record how much cabbage you put in so that you can speed up the process next time. You also need to leave enough space for the cabbage to ferment into – the liquid will increase during fermentation before it subsides again, and you don't want to lose that golden liquid to the bench when it overflows!

So, add about 770 g of cabbage to each 1 litre jar, pressing down one final time to extract the juice. Make sure there is no cabbage on the sides of your jars.

Insert one of the cabbage discs into each jar and press the discs down so that they and all the sauerkraut are well submerged. Now add your weights on top. The liquid should come well up the sides of the weights as you push them down. Close the jars, omitting the rubber seals – the pressure needs to be able to escape from the jars.

Place the jars in a cool room, away from fruit bowls or anything that may have bacterial activity, and leave to ferment for 1–2 weeks. The liquid will increase and bubble and may overflow, so place the jars on a plate or tray. Do not move or open the jars during fermentation.

You will know when the main ferment is complete as the liquid level drops down again and the production of bubbles largely subsides. At this stage, remove the weight and discs, then seal the jars with the rubber seals. Store in the fridge for up to 6 months.

COOK'S NOTES: *Instead of, or in addition to, the caraway seeds, try adding juniper berries, black peppercorns, bay leaves or pepperberries.*

Sprouted Mustards

GEKEIMTER SENF

Making mustard at home is so easy. These versions sprout the mustard seeds first, making them more digestible. You can play around with different flavours once you have the basics down pat, but start with the two combos given here – they are excellent staples to have in your fridge.

MAKES 1 x 500 ML JAR OF EACH MUSTARD
Gluten free / Dairy free / Vegan

Base recipe

- 90 g yellow mustard seeds
- 10 g brown mustard seeds

A good staple mustard

- 2 tsp dried tarragon
- ¼ tsp ground turmeric
- ⅛ tsp ground nutmeg
- ⅛ tsp freshly ground black pepper
- 3 tbsp white wine vinegar
- 2 tsp sea salt flakes

The best ham sandwich mustard

- 1 dried fig
- 2 dried juniper berries
- 1 tbsp ground almonds
- ½ tsp fennel seeds
- ½ tsp coriander seeds
- ¼ tsp ground cinnamon
- ⅛ tsp ground nutmeg
- ⅛ tsp freshly ground black pepper
- 3 tbsp white wine vinegar
- 2 tsp sea salt flakes

Soak the mustard seeds in a generous amount of water at room temperature for 24 hours, or until the seeds are just starting to sprout. Rinse and drain well.

For a good staple mustard, place the soaked mustard seeds in a food processor, reserving ¼ cup if you would like some whole seeds in your mustard. Add the remaining ingredients to the food processor. With the processor running at high speed, slowly add enough warm water until the mustard is a loose paste. It will firm up in the fridge, so add a little more water than your instincts tell you to (this could be anywhere between ¼ cup and ½ cup). Process on high speed for approximately 1 minute.

For the best ham sandwich mustard, place the dried fig and juniper berries in a food processor and blend for a few seconds until finely chopped. Then follow the instructions for a good staple mustard.

Transfer the mustard to a sterilised jar (see page 29 for instructions). Let it sit, with the lid on, on your kitchen bench overnight before tasting. It will be bitter during this time. Store in the fridge for up to 1 year.

ON UGLY MEAT: WHAT OMA KNEW BEST

'When it was broth-making day, us kids would look on out of the corners of our eyes, busying ourselves with other things so that we wouldn't have to go near those big pots of bubbling bones.'

Our grandmother and great-grandmother used to make bone broth as part of their standard cooking routines. Sunday lunch was never served without a plate of clear, rich and deliciously warming chicken broth, and homemade broth was always added to whatever they cooked. Their recipe was simple – carrots chopped in half, a chunk of celeriac, a couple of parsley roots, a large onion and salt went into the pressure cooker with about 4 litres of water, plus whatever meat was on special – a cheap cut of beef, a soup chicken or turkey neck. The meat needed: bone, cartilage, fat, flesh. This was all cooked under pressure, then cooled. The meat would get picked off the bones meticulously – a process that could take half an hour – then our great-grandmother would be presented with the remaining carcass in a soup plate, and she would work any remaining goodness out of it. The extracted vegetables were also never discarded. One of our great-aunts or our grandmother herself would eat these for lunch, as bland as they were. Nothing went to waste.

All our grandparents lived in mainland Europe, albeit in different parts. Throughout their lives, all of them endured hard times, experiencing rationing and food shortages. It made them frugal, clever, industrious and patient. Everything was seen as an opportunity: that chicken neck is good for putting in the soup; these onion skins – what can we do with these? A piece of wire picked up on the street was carefully added to a collection of other found-and-kept items to one day be turned into a knitting needle or a tie to hold together a failed gadget. They took little for granted. They were strong, often stoic, never sitting idly. And the women loved nothing more than to feed their kin.

When it was broth-making day, us kids would look on out of the corners of our eyes, busying ourselves with other things so that we wouldn't have to go near those big pots of bubbling bones or, God forbid, near our great-grandmother in deep concentration over a chicken neck. What we saw was foreign to us. We were growing up in modern, peace-time comfort and what we saw on broth-making days, we *only* saw then and there. Neither our mother nor the mothers of our friends cooked in this way. It was foreign and it was, to some extent, uncomfortable for us. Chicken necks and similar offcuts were disgusting and uncivilised in our eyes. As much as we devoured the broth and loved the sweet smell with which it filled the room, we detested the makings of it. We wanted nothing to do with it.

In a way, this is the affliction of our modern society. What we felt as kids is what many of us feel as adults. We are, by and large, so distanced from the food we eat, especially meat, that we are deeply uncomfortable with anything much more than cutting up a pre-butchered piece of meat for our dinner and cooking it. Even cooking livers is uncomfortable for most of us, let alone chopping the head off a dead chicken. We don't like handling large pieces of fat, organs or obscure cuts that are not on the supermarket shelves.

But these types of meat, much more than the lean and clean cuts, are where so much nourishment is found. In her book, *Real Food for Pregnancy*, US registered dietitian and nutritionist Lily Nichols dedicates a whole section to liver. According to Nichols, liver is the single richest source of iron, one of the richest sources of folate and B12, as well as being incredibly rich in fat-soluble vitamins A, D, E and K. Aside from eggs, it's the only major dietary source of choline. She describes liver as nature's multivitamin. Yet chicken liver, at the time of writing, costs half of what you pay for chicken breast. This is the common story across 'ugly' versus 'pretty' meat. The more nutritionally dense meat is cheaper than the less nutritionally dense. Surely, we should ask why this is the case. Why don't we value ugly meat?

Our great-grandmother was comfortable with killing the chickens she had raised. Her family had fed and housed and cared for these chickens, and she understood that the cycle of life required her to feed her family, and with chicken. She had gone through the rite of passage of killing something in order to eat it – in a way, the ultimate ritual.

In this book, we have purposefully included recipes with ugly meat: Pork Mince Spread (page 81), Schmalz with Crackling (page 80), Chicken Liver Pâté (page 75) and Oma's 24-Hour Chicken Broth (page 55). Preparing, cooking and eating ugly meat, and coming to terms with it, is part of what we need to do to make our food systems more sustainable, transparent and respectful, and to improve our health. We encourage you to take the time to source good-quality ugly meat from the markets or a farm. Ask questions about where it's from and how it was raised. You will find that this is a difficult task when it comes to free-range, organic or regenerative ugly meat – the supply chain is largely not there – but we encourage you to persevere. You might also find, as we do, that your family will be grateful for the offerings of ugly meat you prepare for them. So, feed your kin. Nourish your kin. Find ritual in ugly meat.

Oma's 24-Hour Chicken Broth

OMAS HÜHNERBRÜHE

Growing up, Sunday lunch was always hosted at our Oma's tiny apartment where she lived with our great-grandmother. The aromas greeted us down the hallway before even walking through her door. This recipe was the base of almost every soup, cooked when someone was sick or just as comfort food. Today, my daughters and I read a book about a little bear who heals a little tiger with bouillon and it's what they request when they, too, are unwell. – ***Eva***

MAKES ABOUT 4 LITRES
Gluten free / Dairy free

- 2 raw chicken carcasses
- 1 tbsp apple cider vinegar
- 1 onion or leek, roughly chopped
- 2 carrots, roughly chopped
- 3 celery stalks, roughly chopped
- 1 parsnip, roughly chopped
- 1 turnip, roughly chopped
- bundle of fresh herbs (flat-leaf parsley, lovage and thyme – or whatever soft herbs you have in the garden)
- 1 tsp black peppercorns
- 1 tsp coriander seeds*
- 1 tsp celery seeds*
- 2 dried bay leaves
- fine pink Himalayan salt

SPICE SHORTCUTS*
2 tsp Gewürzhaus Winter Soup Mix

Place all the ingredients except the salt in a large stockpot (I use an 8 litre pot). Fill with water to just cover. Bring to the boil, then reduce to a very low simmer and leave to cook for about 24 hours.

After cooking, allow the broth to cool, then strain the liquid – squeeze the extra liquid out of the vegetables, too. I then pick the meat off the carcasses and give this and the vegetables to our dog, Pretzel. Alternatively, store the meat in an airtight container in the fridge and add it to other meals, and compost the vegetables.

Add salt to taste – I use approximately 1 tablespoon.

Store in the fridge for up to 1 week. If you want to keep the broth for longer, pour into 1 litre sterilised jars (see page 29 for instructions) and heat-treat in a water bath at 100°C for 1 hour (see page 29). Once heat-treated, it will keep for up to 2 years in the pantry.

COOK'S NOTES: *If you are time-poor or feeling unwell, you can easily make this broth in a pressure cooker. Cook for 1 hour from the time the pressure has been reached. Release the steam to bring the pressure down to a safe level before opening the lid. You can also collect vegetable scraps throughout the week in a container in your freezer, and replace some or all of the vegetables with these scraps to make this broth really thrifty.*

Benjamin's Fennel & Lemon Shrub

BENJAMINS FENCHEL-ZITRONEN SHRUB

When my son was little, I was in a dark place. I struggled to find my voice and my rhythm as a continuously sleep-deprived mother. I stopped working for a good while, and during that time, my tonic, and my son's tonic, was time in the veggie garden. We would potter side by side, every day, me planting seedlings, tying up tomato plants or tending to the soil, he picking strawberries, digging in the sandpit or transporting something in his many trucks. After a while, we were grounded in the rhythms of nature. The cycles of day and night, of sunshine and rain, the slowing down of our racing minds, the sound of trees swaying in the breeze. I started observing the moon cycles and watched, in awe, at how my little seedlings would reach their heads up to the big shining full moon in the middle of the night, stretching up and up to meet her pulling force.

In all of that, I was slowly healing, slowly reconnecting with the natural rhythms around me. In the veggie patch, all of the noise was gone. There was no adrenaline or juggling or even demand. I was being shown how to be a mother. Because the secrets of motherhood were right there: to move more slowly, to be more patient, to trust and keep trusting. To understand and believe, in all of your body, that you are enough and that the world requires less of you than you might think.

Often, while we pottered around, I would find my little boy sitting on the path munching fennel, working his way around the bright yellow umbrella of flowers, completely lost in the wonder of what was in his hands.

We still grow fennel today. It self-sows around the veggie patch, its beautiful strong stems reaching up towards the sky, gracing the garden with clusters of yellow and green and then brown seeds. When I see it, I'm reminded of that most difficult and most precious time of my life. And I am overcome with gratitude for being alive and so immensely blessed to be walking this earth. – ***Maria***

MAKES ABOUT 550 ML
Gluten free / Dairy free / Vegetarian

- 10 large fresh fennel flower/seed heads
- peel of 1 lemon, in ribbons (no pith)
- 4 dried pepperberries
- 185 ml (¾ cup) lemon juice
- 185 ml (¾ cup) apple cider vinegar with the mother
- 185 ml (¾ cup) runny honey

Remove the flowers/seeds from their stalks, then pound them in a mortar until they are fragrant. Place them with the lemon peel and pepperberries in a 700 ml–1 litre glass bottle.

Add the remaining ingredients. Seal and shake well until the honey is dissolved. Let the mixture infuse in the fridge for at least 1 week. The flavours will get stronger with time.

When it is to your liking, strain the lot or simply strain off as you use the shrub. Store in the fridge for several months.

To serve, mix a dash of shrub with sparkling water. It's also great with gin or vodka in a mixer. Add a dash to salad dressings or marinades.

COOK'S NOTES: *A shrub is a drinking vinegar, mixed with water like a cordial. Because this shrub uses vinegar with the mother, the bacteria will slowly eat their way through the sugars. After a while, the shrub will turn from its initial sweetness to a more acidic taste. Your shrub is slowly turning into vinegar! If it has progressed too far, you can add more honey, but ideally, don't keep it for too long.*

Breakfast

'On the table in front of us there are platters galore. A plate of cold cuts from the local butcher, filled with Black Forest ham, salami, Italian prosciutto and, my favourite, *Pilzwurst* … Another platter is stacked with soft and hard cheeses from around Europe, and a third with capsicum, cucumber, radishes and other veggies, mostly from the garden. The spaces in between are filled with homemade jams – my favourite here is the cherry jam – and other spreads, such as *quark*, cream cheese, *Schmalz*, pâté and Nutella for the kids.'

Chocolate Semolina Porridge with Morello Cherries

SCHOKO-GRIEẞBREI MIT SAUERKIRSCHEN

Our grandmother would make this for us as our favourite breakfast and comfort food. I remember waking up in the middle of the night in her tiny apartment, where my sister and I top and tailed in a single bed while she slept on the sofa. I couldn't sleep, so at 3 am, she got up and made me *Grießbrei* and I toddled off back to bed. That was the sort of Oma she was. – ***Eva***

SERVES 4
Vegetarian

- 1 litre (4 cups) full-cream milk
- 60 g (½ cup) fine semolina
- 4 tbsp cocoa*
- 1 tsp ground cassia*
- 2 tbsp coconut sugar
- 1 × 680 g jar pitted morello cherries, drained but liquid reserved

SPICE SHORTCUTS*
4 tbsp + 1 tsp Gewürzhaus Feel Good Hot Chocolate or Gewürzhaus Chocolate Spice

Warm the milk in a saucepan over medium heat. When it is close to a simmer, add the semolina, whisking briskly so that no clumps form. Add the cocoa, cassia and sugar and whisk until combined. Cook over medium–low heat for 2–3 minutes, whisking continuously, until the mixture thickens.

To serve, divide the hot porridge among four bowls and spoon the cherries on top. Drizzle with some of the reserved cherry liquid.

With the remaining cherry liquid, you can make a delicious shrub. Follow the recipe on page 192, replacing the rhubarb with the cherry liquid and adding a few star anise to the bottle.

If you have leftover porridge, store it in an airtight container in the fridge for a few days and eat it cold or reheat in the microwave.

One-Pan Farmer's Breakfast

DEFTIGES BAUERNFRÜHSTÜCK

This dish was traditionally served to farmers in the mornings to give them energy and fill them up for the hard day's labour ahead. These days, it is a staple in German households and is not only served for breakfast, but also for lunches or at dinner with a beer in hand. It is often made with leftover potatoes and other vegetables from last night's dinner.

SERVES 4
Gluten free

1 kg waxy potatoes (such as kipfler, desiree or nicola), skin on and washed

200 g bacon rashers, rind removed, cut into 5 mm × 1 cm pieces

40 g salted butter

2 tbsp extra-virgin olive oil

2 onions, quartered and sliced

4 eggs

2½ tbsp full-cream milk

½ tsp sweet paprika*

¼ tsp ground nutmeg*

½ tsp fine Himalayan pink salt*

⅛ tsp freshly cracked black pepper*

To serve

chopped parsley and chives

sour gherkin, cut into a fan (optional)

SPICE SHORTCUTS*
1½ tsp Gewürzhaus Bratkartoffel Spice

Add the potatoes to a large saucepan of cold water. Bring to the boil and cook until you can insert a skewer into the potatoes with little resistance, about 15–20 minutes. Drain and cool until lukewarm. Peel and set aside to cool completely.

In a large frying pan over high heat, fry the bacon until crispy, about 5 minutes. Depending on how fatty the bacon is, you may need a little olive oil to help grease the pan. Remove the bacon from the pan and set aside.

Add half the butter and half the oil to the pan and cook the onion over medium heat until translucent, about 5 minutes. Remove the onion from the pan and set aside.

Cut the potatoes in half, then cut into 1 cm thick slices.

Add the remaining butter and oil to the pan and, when melted, add the potato. Cook over high heat until it becomes crispy, carefully turning a couple of times. You may need a little more oil if the potato sticks.

Meanwhile, whisk the eggs, milk, spices, salt and pepper together.

Reduce the heat to medium–low, return the bacon and onion to the pan and gently mix them through the potato.

Pour the egg mixture evenly over the potato, pressing the potato into the egg mixture. Cook over low heat until just set, about 15 minutes. Sprinkle with the parsley and chives and place the gherkin, if using, in the centre of the pan. Serve at the table while hot.

COOK'S NOTES: *If you have an ovenproof pan, you can also set the egg in the oven at 180°C for 10–15 minutes, rather than on the stovetop, to minimise the risk of the underside burning.*

Gingerbread Honey Cereal

GEPUFFTES LEBKUCHEN MÜSLI

This cereal is Christmas in a bowl. Add milk, some sliced banana if you fancy, and the whole family will sing your praises *and* be fuelled for the day's adventures. It appears deceptively light in texture and oh-so moreish, yet, as you will discover when you throw it together, it's full of fats and proteins that will ward off mid-morning cravings and toddler tantrums. A gift to yourself and everyone eating it. – ***Maria***

MAKES 2 × 2 LITRE JARS
Gluten free / Dairy free / Vegetarian

12 cups popped gluten-free grains (use a mix of brown rice, millet, corn, buckwheat, quinoa, amaranth or similar)

60 g (1 cup) shredded coconut

100 g (1 cup) ground almonds

170 g (¾ cup) coconut oil

240 g (¾ cup) honey

1 tbsp ground cassia*

1 tbsp ground coriander seeds*

3½ tsp ground star anise*

3½ tsp ground ginger*

1½ tsp ground nutmeg*

⅛ tsp fine rock salt

SPICE SHORTCUTS*
4 tbsp Gewürzhaus Gingerbread Spice, Gewürzhaus Hot Cross Bun Spice, Gewürzhaus St Nicholas Spekulaas Spice or Gewürzhaus Christmas Cake & Pudding Spice

Preheat the oven to 160°C conventional. Line a large sheet pan (approximately 40 cm × 30 cm).

Combine the dry ingredients in the sheet pan.

In a saucepan over low heat, melt the oil, honey, spices and salt, stirring continuously until well combined and liquid. Pour the mixture over the dry ingredients in the sheet pan and mix through thoroughly with a large spoon. Bake in the oven for 15–20 minutes.

For clusters, let the mixture cool completely, then break into chunks. If you prefer loose grains, stir the mixture occasionally as it cools. Store in two 2 litre jars or a large airtight container in the pantry for several months.

0.5 Liter

BASIL
THYME
CASSIA
ALLSPICE
BAY

Blackberry & Basil Honey Jam

BROMBEER-HONIG-MARMELADE MIT BASILIKUM

We are so lucky to live on a beautiful plot of land where many things grow. This recipe came about from a summer stroll through the garden, collecting what was ripe in my upturned straw hat: a few handfuls of blackberries, juicy plums, loads of basil, fresh thyme, some fallen lemons and a lone, last orange on the tree. It's sweetened with just a little honey; sweet, sun-ripened fruit doesn't need more than that. It has become one of our favourites and I love watching the kids tuck into it on fresh sourdough, their little mouths outlined with traces of the summer's harvest, blackberry seeds stuck in their teeth. – ***Maria***

MAKES ABOUT 700 ML
Gluten free / Dairy free / Vegetarian

- 650 g blackberries
- 200 g stoned plums, halved
- 1 bunch of basil, leaves picked
- ½ bunch of thyme, leaves picked
- 1 orange, peeled and roughly chopped
- 1½ tsp ground cassia*
- ¼ tsp ground allspice*
- ⅛ tsp ground cloves*
- ⅛ tsp ground bay leaf (or use a whole dried leaf, but add it after blending and remove before adding the honey)
- ⅛ tsp fine Himalayan pink salt
- 130 g (½ cup) medium-strength honey
- 2 tbsp lemon juice

SPICE SHORTCUTS*
2 tsp Gewürzhaus Mixed Spice

Place all the ingredients, except the honey and lemon juice, in a food processor. Add 1 tablespoon of water and blend for about 1 minute.

Transfer to a medium, heavy-based saucepan and bring to a simmer over medium heat, stirring regularly. Reduce the heat slightly so that the fruit is cooking at a low simmer. Cook for about 1 hour in total or until the fruit has thickened and cooked down by about one-third. Stir regularly, especially towards the end of cooking, making sure the jam isn't sticking to the bottom of the pan.

Add the honey and lemon juice and stir in well. Cook for a further 10 minutes, stirring regularly.

Transfer the jam to small, sterilised jars (see page 29 for instructions) and heat-treat in a water bath at 90°C for 30 minutes (see page 29).

Store in the pantry for 1–2 years. Once opened, store in the fridge for several weeks and make sure you only use a clean spoon to dig into the jar, as the sugar content is low and mould will form more easily than in conventional jam.

COOK'S NOTES: *You can use a Thermomix to make this jam. Cook the processed fruit for 60 mins/90°C/speed 2, uncovered, and then for a further 10 mins/90°C/speed 2.5 after you have added the honey. Easy peasy.*

THE GERMAN BREAKFAST TABLE

'When we all sit together, we catch up slowly and eventually make plans for the day ahead. It's such a calm and beautiful way to start the day and our trip, and it's always a highlight for everyone.'

One of my favourite things about travelling to Germany for holidays is the *Frühstückstisch* (breakfast table) and the way that Germans eat breakfast. Ironically, at home in Melbourne, I don't eat breakfast at all. In everyday life I'm generally too rushed and so somehow just not hungry. Fast forward to our next German vacation and I'll be converted for the duration of the trip.

We usually land in Munich as it's the closest airport to the place I was born, the tiny village of Hürben in Baden-Württemberg. Here, our beautiful family friends, Helga and Friedel, live in a house with a morning sun–facing terrace and the most beautiful garden. While it's not our home, it feels like it: comforting, familiar and filled with love. This is almost always our first stop when we arrive. We hire a fast (German) car, so that we can enjoy the *Autobahn* (freeway), where the speed limit is as fast as you feel comfortable with. This gives me so much joy and this particular stretch of *Autobahn* is heavenly to drive.

Our flight often arrives early and we get to Hürben with the terrace table set and awaiting us. It looks so inviting, full of food placed with care, and we all pause to marvel at what is laid out in front of us. Excited, we sit down and work out what to have first. Helga appears with freshly brewed coffee from the drip coffee machine, a staple in every German household. The coffee smells and tastes different here from back in Australia, and the first sip helps us to fight the jetlag and fatigue from the long flight.

On the table in front of us there are platters galore. A plate of cold cuts from the local butcher, filled with Black Forest ham, salami, Italian prosciutto and, my favourite, *Pilzwurst*, which can be best described as a mortadella with champignons. Another platter is stacked with soft and hard cheeses from around Europe, and a third with capsicum, cucumber, radishes and other veggies, mostly from the garden. The spaces in between are filled with homemade jams – my favourite here is the cherry jam – and other spreads, such as *quark*, cream cheese, *Schmalz*, pâté and Nutella for the kids. There would be an uproar if they forgot Mum's favourite *Fleischsalat*, which loosely translates to 'meat salad', the main ingredient being a meat similar to mortadella, which is cut into strips and combined with gherkins and a whole-egg mayonnaise. It's more of a spread, but you can also eat it by the spoonful, it's that delicious.

Then comes the best part … the bread. Our hosts will visit two local bakeries in the morning to buy a variety of fresh bread rolls at the first, making sure they include my favourite *Laugenbrötchen* (lye bread rolls) and Mum's favourite *Zwiebelbrötchen* (onion bread rolls). Next, they will go to the second bakery because there you get the best *Brezeln* (pretzels), which the kids love the most. There are at least a dozen different rolls and baked goods for us to choose from.

Everything is bought from small local stores or is homemade, and is presented with care and detail – the salami is rolled up, the bread rolls are in a basket lined with an ironed napkin, the crockery is perfectly matching.

When we all sit together, we catch up slowly and eventually make plans for the day ahead. It's such a calm and beautiful way to start the day and our trip, and it's always a highlight for everyone.

Perhaps the best part is that this is not just a special welcome breakfast, this happens EVERY DAY! And not just at Helga and Friedel's house, for almost the entire trip, this will be our morning ritual, prepared by our friends and relatives all over the country. How very special.

– Eva

CLOCKWISE FROM TOP LEFT: GERMAN ONION RYE BREAD (PAGE 76), LYE PRETZELS (PAGE 82), CHICKEN LIVER PÂTÉ (PAGE 73), SCHMALZ WITH CRACKLING (PAGE 80), BLACKBERRY & BASIL HONEY JAM (PAGE 66), SALTED ORANGE MARMALADE (PAGE 90), PORK MINCE SPREAD (PAGE 81) ON TOAST

JUNIPER
NUTMEG
ALLSPICE
THYME

Chicken Liver Pâté

LEBERPASTETE

The recipe for this pâté came from the Ross family of amazing cooks. My friend Stuart, whom I was going to credit, insisted that it was his mother, Joyce, who deserved the glory. I have been making it for years and have had friends ask for the recipe just like I did when I first tried it. Like most recipes I get handed down, I find ways to incorporate spices into them and in this, too, I have added juniper berries, allspice and orange peel. So, if you're wanting to try the OG recipe, then omit these. Joyce also capped the pâté, once refrigerated, with either melted butter or a gelatine mixture. – ***Eva***

MAKES 2 × 500 ML JARS
Gluten free

- 500 g chicken livers (organic if possible), washed
- 125 ml (½ cup) port
- 100 g salted butter
- 2 French shallots, finely chopped
- 1 garlic clove, crushed
- 1 tsp thyme leaves
- 10 juniper berries, crushed*
- ¼ tsp ground nutmeg*
- ¼ tsp ground allspice*
- ½ tsp orange peel powder*
- 80 ml (⅓ cup) cream
- 1 tsp sea salt flakes

SPICE SHORTCUTS*
1½ tsp Gewürzhaus Goddess of Hunting Spice

Put the chicken livers in a bowl, cover with the port and refrigerate overnight.

Drain the livers and reserve the port. Some recipes prefer to trim the livers, although if you have a powerful food processor, I personally think it's fine to skip this step. Not only does it save time, you also use everything instead of creating waste.

Melt half the butter in a small saucepan over low heat until it begins to foam. Add the shallot, garlic, thyme, spices and orange peel powder and sauté until soft but not brown, about 5–7 minutes. Increase the heat to high and add the livers. Cook for about 4 minutes. Add the port to deglaze the pan and cook for a further minute.

Remove the pan from the stove and transfer the contents to a food processor. Add the cream, salt and remaining butter and blend on high until you have a smooth purée.

At this point, you can choose to pass the mixture through a sieve for a very smooth pâté, but I never bother.

Pour into a serving bowl or lidded glass containers. Let it cool completely before covering or sealing. The pâté will keep in the fridge for 1 week.

COOK'S NOTES: *If you have the freezer space, you can quadruple this recipe and freeze it in small batches. Simply defrost in the fridge when you need more.*

German Onion Rye Bread

ZWIEBEL-ROGGENBROT

Zwiebelbrot is one of my mum's favourite breads from Germany, one she misses a great deal. I make this for her occasionally to enjoy with good butter or *Schmalz*. It has a deliciously nutty, salty–sweet flavour and it's completely worth the effort of making it. – ***Maria***

MAKES 1 LARGE LOAF
Vegetarian

Leaven

20 g active sourdough starter

50 g stoneground rye flour

50 g water

Onion

knob of salted butter

1 large onion, halved and sliced

pinch of fine Himalayan pink salt

Dough

240 g stoneground rye flour

360 g stoneground unbleached baker's wheat flour, plus extra for dusting

1 tsp caraway seeds

450 g warm water #1

60 g warm water #2

15 g fine Himalayan pink salt

To make the leaven, feed the starter with the flour and water the night before you make your dough. Mix it well. Cover and leave it on the kitchen bench at room temperature overnight.

The following day, prepare the onion. Melt the butter in a large, heavy-based saucepan over medium heat. When it is hot, stir through the onion and salt. Cook and stir for 10–12 minutes, until the onion is browned and starting to get some crunch, but not too dark in colour. Set aside to cool completely.

To make the dough, place the flours and caraway in a large bowl and mix well. Add the warm water #1 and bring the dough together, first with a fork and then with wet hands. Don't knead at this stage – you are just 'wetting' the dough. Set aside, covered with a damp tea towel, to autolyse for 30 minutes.

Add the warm water #2, salt, leaven and onion to the dough. Knead and squeeze these into the dough well, for about 2–3 minutes. Clean your hands, then wet them and start folding the dough from the edge into the centre. Work your way around the dough a few times, continuing to wet your hands as you go. Cover and set aside for 45 minutes.

Do a stretch and fold: wet your hands, then scoop under one part of the dough with one hand, then stretch it up as far as you can. Use the other hand to steady the bowl, or even to help hold down the bulk of the dough if your dough is a bit stiff. Place the stretched dough down onto the remaining dough. Repeat this on the opposite side. Now turn the bowl 90 degrees and do another set of stretch and folds with the remaining two sides of the dough. Carefully lift the dough with both hands and flip it upside down.

Next, do a small coil fold: scoop up the entire dough by placing your hands under opposite sides of the dough and stretching it up in the middle until the dough is no longer touching the bowl, like a sloppy bridge. Lower it back down, letting the ends fold under the bulk of the dough, giving you a coil of some sort. Set aside, covered, for 45 minutes.

CONTINUED OVERLEAF >

Do another stretch and fold, flip and coil fold. Cover and set aside for 45 minutes.

Do another stretch and fold, flip and coil fold. Cover and set aside for 45 minutes.

Do another stretch and fold, flip and coil fold. Cover and set aside for 1 hour.

Turn the dough out onto a clean bench. Ideally, don't flour the bench but, if the dough is too sticky for you to handle, you can lightly flour it. Do a lamination: stretch the dough out into all directions as far as you can – you should end up with a rough square/rectangle. This helps to develop the structure of the dough. Don't worry if the shape is wonky or the dough rips a little. Then fold the edge furthest away from you onto the edge closest to you – like a greeting card. Next, fold the left edge onto the right, then the right onto the left, making three folds in total. The dough should end up being roughly the same size as it was in the bowl.

Now, pre-shape the dough: carefully lift the dough with both hands and turn it upside down. Shape the dough by pulling it towards you with a dough scraper, held at an angle. You are trying to form a ball and get tension across the top of it, so place the scraper just at the spot where the dough is touching the bench and pull it swiftly towards you. Keep moving the dough around the bench with your scraper, from all four 'sides', until you have a tight ball. Rest for 20 minutes, uncovered.

Lay a clean tea towel over a large bowl and sprinkle generously with flour.

Flip the dough over and flatten it out a little, to give you a small square, about 25 cm. Fold one edge into the middle, then repeat with the opposite edge. Now fold the other two edges into the middle. Flip it again, then work it into a tight ball with your dough scraper, as for the pre-shape. Flour the top of the ball, then transfer it onto the tea towel and into the bowl by quickly and confidently pushing the scraper under one side of the ball, supporting it on the opposite side with your hand. Flip it into the supporting hand and place the dough, floured-side down, onto the tea towel. Sprinkle more flour around the edges of the dough and onto the top. Loosely cover the dough with the overhanging tea towel, then place it into a large, hole-free plastic bag and seal. Rest for a further 20 minutes before placing the bowl on the lowest shelf of your fridge to proof overnight.

The next day, place a large enamelled cast-iron casserole pot with a lid in the oven and preheat to 250°C fan-forced. Generously flour a piece of stiff cardboard – I use the flattened lid of an old pizza box, folded down the middle.

When the oven has reached temperature, flour the top of the dough again, then turn it out gently onto the cardboard by upending the bowl. Score the top of the loaf with a sharp knife – a new serrated, rounded kitchen knife works a treat for this and you can keep it separate for just this purpose. If you are going to bake a lot, you can invest in a bread-scoring lame for this purpose. Score the bread with 10 cm long cuts from the inside out – make a sort of rose-petal pattern.

Transfer the hot pot from the oven onto a heatproof trivet on the kitchen floor. Remove the lid, then gently but quickly slide the bread into the pot. Replace the lid, place the pot in the oven and bake for 30 minutes. Remove the lid and bake, uncovered, for a further 5 minutes.

Remove the bread from the pot – you can use tongs to help – then let it cool completely on a wire rack. Let the bread cure for 5–8 hours if you can wait that long. It is worth it, as the loaf will fully develop its flavour in this time and stay fresh for longer once cut.

COOK'S NOTES: *This recipe uses stoneground flours, which are more absorbent than commercially ground bleached baker's flours. You will have to adjust the amount of water if you use different flours.*

SCHMALZ WITH CRACKLING (PAGE 80) ON GERMAN ONION RYE BREAD

Schmalz with Crackling

GRIEBENSCHMALZ

Schmalz on fresh bread is hard to beat, with its flavours of sautéed onion, fennel and apple, as well as the crunchy crackling in its midst. When we were kids, we had this regularly with chopped chives for breakfast. I love that it is made with a part of the animal that many people would throw out – the fat. – ***Maria***

MAKES ABOUT 900 ML
Gluten free / Dairy free

- 1 kg cold pork fat (either leaf or back fat)
- 1 onion, semi-finely chopped (optional)
- 1 apple, peeled, cored and semi-finely chopped (optional)
- 14 g fine Himalayan pink salt per kg of pork fat*
- 2 tsp crushed fennel seeds*
- 2 tsp dried marjoram*
- pinch of freshly cracked black pepper*

SPICE SHORTCUTS*
1 tbsp Gewürzhaus Crunchy Pork Crackling Rub, plus 10 g fine Himalayan pink salt

Prepare the fat by passing it through a meat grinder or chopping it into 1 cm cubes with a sharp knife. Small amounts of meat and skin can also be chopped. Your butcher might grind it for you, otherwise put some music on and enjoy the methodical nature of this task. Weigh the fat and note this down, then place it in a pot with a spout – I use a 2 litre enamel measuring jug.

To render the fat, heat it on the smallest burner over the lowest heat for 10 minutes. Stir, cook for another 10 minutes, then turn up the heat to medium–low. Keep cooking, stirring at 10-minute intervals. When there is a decent amount of liquid fat in the pot (after about 40 minutes), pour it into a bowl or large measuring jug, using a spatula or wooden spoon to hold back the solids. Return to the heat and continue cooking, stirring and pouring off. Turn down the heat again if necessary.

In the meantime, if you are adding the onion and apple, pour 5 mm of the liquid fat into a frying pan over medium heat. Add the onion and apple. Stir well, making sure they are saturated in the fat. Cook for 20 minutes, stirring regularly – and in the last 5 minutes stirring continuously – to make sure nothing burns. When the onion and apple are nicely browned, transfer to the vessel containing the liquid fat.

After about 1 hour and 40 minutes of rendering the fat, the solids will be dried out and will have turned into crackling. Take extra care towards the end of the cooking time that the crackling doesn't burn. When the solids have largely stopped releasing oil, transfer them to a large plate and sprinkle with salt. Set aside to cool and harden.

In the meantime, add the salt, fennel, marjoram and pepper to the liquid fat. Stir and set aside to cool. When the fat starts to turn white and solidify – when the spices are submerged rather than sinking to the bottom – give it a good whip, then stir in the crackling. You don't need to add it all, you can sprinkle it on just about anything or eat it straight from the plate.

Pour or spoon the *Schmalz* into sterilised jars (see page 29 for instructions) and store in the fridge for several months.

Pork Mince Spread

METT

My great friend, Franz Kiel, started the tradition of an annual sausage-making day with our group of friends here in Melbourne. Each year, in winter, we get together to light the fire, make mulled wine, drink German beer, listen to the song Johnny Däpp on repeat, while cutting up meat and weighing out spices to mix together various recipes to make sausages. In his hand luggage, Franz schlepped back the heavy mincer and the sausage filler from Germany, which I'm sure have more technical names, such was the desire to bring this tradition to Australia. Each of our friends brings some other food to share and we spend the afternoon and long evening together. Every year, it is always very special and highly anticipated in the calendar. The entrée for a few of us is always *Mett*, which just happens to be a biproduct of making sausages. There is not much to get wrong, and as long as the meat is fresh and the salt content is correct, most spice combinations you would use in sausage making yield a delicious *Mett*. We make sure we've bought a crunchy sourdough baguette and then spread the freshly minced mixture onto the sliced bread to the great disgust of many of our friends. If you like beef tartare or carpaccio, this might be the dish for you. – ***Eva***

SERVES 8
Gluten free / Dairy free

- 300 g boneless pork shoulder, roughly diced
- 200 g skinless pork belly, roughly diced
- 9 g fine Himalayan pink salt
- ½ tsp dried marjoram
- ¼ tsp dried parsley
- ¼ tsp ground mace
- ¼ tsp crushed cumin seeds
- ¼ tsp crushed fennel seeds
- ⅛ tsp ground allspice
- ⅛ tsp freshly cracked black pepper
- ½ small onion, finely chopped
- 1 garlic clove, crushed

Put the pork in a bowl, add the salt, dried herbs and spices, then toss together. Put this through a mincer using the fine disc, or if you don't have a mincer, very briefly pulse it in a food processor until it is a coarse, mince-like consistency. It should have texture and not become a paste.

Add the onion and garlic and mix them through the pork. With your hands, mash everything together until well combined and somewhat emulsified.

Spread the *Mett* on crusty bread and eat it raw. Consume the *Mett* on the same day you make it.

COOK'S NOTES: *Ask your butcher for pork that is as freshly butchered as possible.*

Lye Pretzels

LAUGENBREZELN

In Australia, it is very difficult to find delicious *Brezeln*, so a while ago, I decided to dedicate some time to learning how to make them myself. I'll admit, at first it was pretty daunting: the lye solution, the yeast dough, the shaping. It is all quite the process, but if you enjoy bread making or cooking from scratch, then you won't be a stranger to slow processes and will find joy in the creating. It is possible to use baking soda, however, the traditional lye solution gives the chewy crust, glossy sheen and golden colour, not to mention a specific taste that is unmistakable. Traditionally, there are two methods of pretzel shaping depending on the region of Germany. The one we grew up with has a thicker belly, a larger loop and thin crossed arms. One part becomes soft and fluffy when baked and the other is thin and crunchy. This is how I like to make them. – ***Eva***

MAKES 8
Vegetarian

- 500 g (3⅓ cups) plain flour, plus extra for dusting
- 40 g fresh yeast
- 2 tsp white sugar
- 1¼ tsp fine Himalayan pink salt
- 50 g salted butter, softened
- pretzel salt, for sprinkling

Lye bath

- 30 g food-grade lye

SAFETY NOTE: *Lye (sodium hydroxide) is caustic and should be used with caution. It can cause chemical burns and may induce blindness if it comes into contact with the eyes. Wear protective equipment, such as rubber gloves and eye protection. Lye is corrosive to some metals so protect any benches with a plastic cloth.*

Place the flour in a mixing bowl and create a well in the centre. Crumble the yeast into the well and add 140 ml of lukewarm water, the sugar and salt. Gently mix these together, incorporating a little of the flour as you go. Sprinkle a thin layer of flour over the water, cover the bowl with a damp tea towel and place in a warm spot for 20 minutes. After this time, the yeast should be bubbling. Add another 140 ml of lukewarm water and the butter and mix with a fork, working from the inside out, slowly incorporating all the flour. Once it becomes too difficult to mix with the fork, use your hands to scoop up the dough from the outside and fold it into the centre. Once the dough starts coming together, turn it out onto a lightly floured bench and knead it into a soft and silky dough for about 5–7 minutes.

Flour a clean bowl, lightly rub the dough in oil, then place the dough in the bowl, dust with flour again and cover with a damp tea towel. Place in a warm spot for 1 hour.

After an hour, the dough should have doubled in size. Turn it out onto a lightly floured bench and gently knead. The dough should be elastic and if you press your finger into it, it should spring back once removed.

CONTINUED OVERLEAF >

Cut the dough into eight pieces (about 100 g each). Roll each piece into a 60 cm long rope, with the centre about the thickness of your thumb and the ends tapering off to the thickness of a pencil. Depending on how quickly you work, you may want to cover the other dough balls with a damp tea towel so they don't dry out – do not flour them, otherwise they will become very hard to roll out.

Now it's time to form the pretzels. Take the ends of one rope into each hand and form an upside-down 'U' shape. Next, twist the strands over each other twice. Bring the two ends down towards the bottom of the pretzel and press them into the body. You should have a pretzel with one big hole and two smaller holes. Repeat to make eight pretzels. Place the pretzels on a lined baking tray. Let the pretzels rest for 15 minutes, then place them in the fridge for 30 minutes. Placing them in the fridge hardens them, making it much easier to dip them into the lye bath without them deforming.

To make the lye bath, first read the safety instructions on page 82. Pour 1 litre (4 cups) of cold water into a large stainless-steel, glass or plastic bowl, then add the lye. Mix with a plastic or stainless-steel utensil until the mixture turns from milky to clear.

Preheat the oven to 200°C fan-forced.

Take the pretzels out of the fridge and, wearing gloves, dip each one in the lye bath for 15 seconds. Remove and allow the lye to drip off. Place them back on the lined tray. Repeat until all the pretzels are done. Cut little slits into the fat parts of the pretzels and sprinkle all over with pretzel salt.

Bake for 15–20 minutes. Remove the pretzels from the oven and eat while hot, with lashings of good butter.

The pretzels are best eaten on the day they are made. If you have any that have become too hard, dry them out completely, then turn them into uniquely delicious breadcrumbs.

COOK'S NOTES: *You can purchase food-grade lye online in powder or pearl form. Some bakeries also sell it. These lye pretzels can be frozen. To do this, omit the pretzel salt before baking and take them out of the oven about 5 minutes early. Let them cool, then freeze. When you are ready to eat them, moisten them with a little water, sprinkle with pretzel salt and cook for 5 minutes in a 200°C fan-forced oven – no need to thaw first.*

MAKING MARMALADE

'Among all of this slumber, though, there is life. Three trees, to be exact. All covered in wonderfully bright yellow and orange balls, in the company of lush, green leaves.'

Where we live, winters are cold. Not arctic, not bitterly cold, but cold enough for big frosts and woollen scarves. We have defined seasons, and each brings us a different thing to look forward to. That's something I've really come to appreciate since moving from the city to the quasi-country, where our big garden produces an array of different fruit and vegetables through the seasons.

In winter, especially late winter, the days are short but can seem really long. The garden is cold and brown; the deciduous plants are hibernating in their wood, the colours of autumn long gone; there might be rain and clouds, the kids' gumboots wet inside and out; the late-summer pumpkins are well and truly picked and stored in the garage; the winter veg – cauliflowers, cabbages, onions, maybe some carrots – seem to be on pause after their short-lived scramble for the sun's remaining rays.

Among all of this slumber, though, there is life. Three trees, to be exact. All covered in wonderfully bright yellow and orange balls, in the company of lush, green leaves. A tangelo, a grapefruit and an orange tree. These trees, adorned like Christmas trees with their fruit, are shining beacons in the gloomy landscape.

We gather baskets, don raincoats and gumboots and head out. There is a real delight in plucking citrus from a tree. Children understand this inherently. Their little faces are overjoyed when they manage to pull off a tangelo, the oil in its skin gently misting their noses with its life-affirming scent. Citrus is a tonic for our winter psyches.

We fill our baskets and head back inside, peeling off our layers like onions. The kids are then set up in the laundry where they juice their harvest. My son especially loves this task. He will chip away at it until a jug is full, then proudly present it to the family. Then he and his sister fill cups and inhale the sour-sweet juice – the best vitamin C boost they can get – and all right there in nature, provided exactly when we need it.

In the meantime, my mum and I prepare our harvest for making marmalade. The fruit is scrubbed and weighed, then we start the methodical task of carefully slicing each piece into thin segments. We sit around the kitchen table and chat, our hands busy and our minds purposefully occupied. I enjoy this time together; there's a peaceful connection that forms between two people who are quietly engaged in the same thing. Like laughing at a movie together.

When the chopping is done, the fruit goes into the big stockpot to cook and we make another mug of coffee. The house begins to fill with the fragrance of citrus and spices, and on this day we all feel like winter is fine, actually. It's not really that long or cold or monotone, is it?

– Maria

CARDAMOM
CLOVE
JUNIPER
ROSEMARY
GINGER

Salted Orange Marmalade with Cardamom, Juniper Berry & Rosemary

GESALZENE ORANGENMARMELADE MIT KARDAMOM, WACHOLDERBEEREN UND ROSMARIN

My friend Graham gifted me a jar of his homemade cardamom and rosemary marmalade, complete with a dash of whiskey, and I have been making a version of his recipe ever since, with the abundance of citrus that grows every winter in my garden. I love the bitterness of the grapefruit and the sourness of the tangelo to balance out the sweetness of the orange; the spices add various flavour complexities. Altogether, this is one moreish and addictive marmalade. – ***Maria***

MAKES ABOUT 3 LITRES
Gluten free / Dairy free / Vegan

- 1 kg oranges (about 8)
- 1 kg tangelos (about 8)
- 250 ml (1 cup) grapefruit juice (from about 5 grapefruit)
- 1 tbsp cardamom pods
- ½ tsp cloves
- 6 dried juniper berries
- 1.5 kg raw sugar
- 1 tsp fine Himalayan pink salt
- 2 rosemary sprigs, leaves picked and chopped
- 1 tsp ground ginger
- ¼ tsp freshly cracked black pepper

Scrub the oranges and tangelos well and cut away any blemishes from the peel. Cut each one in half lengthways, then slice finely. Cut the slices into thirds so you have small segments. Remove any pips and place in the compost.

Place the fruit in a large stockpot. Add the grapefruit juice, 3.5 litres of water, the cardamom, cloves and juniper berries. Cook over medium–low heat, covered, for 30 minutes or until the peel is softened. Make sure the mixture is not boiling or simmering.

Add the sugar and stir until it is completely dissolved. Add the salt, increase the heat to high and cook at a rolling boil for 1½–2 hours, stirring occasionally. Reduce to about 3.5 litres, or to a stage when the marmalade is starting to thicken. Skim off the spices if you like – I leave them in.

Reduce the liquid further over high heat until the marmalade is bubbling vigorously and splattering up the side of the pot and is becoming quite thick. Stir frequently so your marmalade doesn't stick to the base and burn. Add the rosemary, ginger and pepper and stir them through.

There are several methods to determine the set of your marmalade. The nuances of flavour tend to shine more when the marmalade is still a bit runny; the right set is about finding the point where the marmalade is just thick enough so the flavours are at their best.

CONTINUED OVERLEAF >

Temperature-wise, this is somewhere just above 100°C (say 103°C). If you have a candy thermometer, use it to reach this point. Otherwise, test it as my mum does. Cook the marmalade until you feel it is about right. Turn the heat off. Place a ladleful of marmalade into a small bowl or jar and cover. Put the remaining marmalade in the pot in a cool place. Then make yourself a coffee and enjoy the afternoon! The next morning, make some buttered toast and dollop some of the cold marmalade from the bowl on it. Is the consistency to your liking? Does it taste good? If yes, put the pot back on the stove and slowly heat the marmalade, stirring occasionally. Increase the heat to high until the marmalade is hot, then pour into warm sterilised jars (see page 29 for instructions) and seal with the lids.

Store in the pantry for 1 year and refrigerate after opening. Use only a clean knife or spoon to dip into the marmalade – it is more prone to mould as there is slightly less sugar than in regular marmalade.

COOK'S NOTES: *You will need a large 9–10 litre heavy-based stockpot to make this quantity. Halve the recipe if you don't have one.*

Mains

'Once the fondue pot with hot broth was placed on the base with the flame lit, surrounded by accompanying platters, everyone loaded their forks and started cooking. It was a beautiful, interactive and slow way to enjoy food, often going on until midnight. We remember these evenings with great fondness: different generations sitting around a table, sharing food and stories.'

Crepe Soup

FLÄDLESUPPE

Another simple and flavoursome dish from our home region of Swabia in the south of Germany. It is a great appetiser for a winter dinner party, being not too filling and presenting beautifully on the table. If you have kids who detest greens, you can also omit these, though the idea of pancakes in soup is generally well received. – ***Eva***

SERVES 4

2.5 litres Oma's 24-Hour Chicken Broth (page 55)

Crepes

4 eggs

150 g (1 cup) plain flour

½ tsp ground nutmeg*

¼ tsp ground cinnamon*

¼ tsp ground white pepper*

1 tsp sea salt flakes

250 ml (1 cup) full-cream milk

¼ cup flat-leaf parsley leaves, finely chopped

¼ cup chives, finely chopped

salted butter, for frying

SPICE SHORTCUTS*

1 tsp Gewürzhaus Quatre Épices

Heat the broth in a saucepan over medium heat, covered, until it is just simmering. Season to taste.

In the meantime, make the crepes. Whisk the eggs in a bowl and mix in the flour, spices and salt until you have a smooth paste. Slowly add the milk, whisking to incorporate until there are no lumps. Mix in the fresh herbs.

Heat a lightly buttered wide frying pan over medium heat. Pour or scoop just enough mixture to cover the base of the pan. Immediately tip and rotate the pan to spread the batter as thinly as possible. Cook for 1–2 minutes until lightly brown, then flip and cook for a further minute. Transfer to a plate while you cook the remaining crepes. Continue until all the batter is used up.

Roll up each crepe, then cut into 5 mm wide strips. Divide the rolled crepes among soup bowls, while trying to keep them rolled up, then ladle the hot broth over the top.

Store leftover pancakes in an airtight container in the fridge for a few days.

Oma Rosa's Gulasch

OMA ROSAS GULASCH

Our great-grandmother, Rosa, was the head chef of the gaggle of women on our dad's side, who all lived within a stone's throw of each other in the town of Goslar in the north of Germany, where Eva and I spent our winter holidays as kids. She had an old armchair positioned at the kitchen entrance in the tiny apartment she shared with our Oma Liesel. That is where she sat, in her black clothing that didn't seem to change, knitting socks and giving orders to her daughters in the kitchen. She was sharp as a needle right until her last day, tasting every dish that came out of that kitchen, always with the final word on what was missing. This *Gulasch* was on heavy rotation, cooked in a big pressure cooker that would fill the apartment in fragrant steam. Its flavour comes from the quality and freshness of the paprika, something our Omas always had on hand, procured from someone who knew someone who had been back to their place of birth, near the Hungarian border in Romania. It's a recipe we both still cook regularly today, and when asked which spice blend most embodies what Gewürzhaus is about, we say Oma Rosa's Gulasch. – ***Maria***

SERVES 8
Gluten free (if using GF cornflour)

- 3 tbsp extra-virgin olive oil
- 5 onions, halved and finely sliced
- 1¾ tbsp Hungarian noble sweet (édesnemes) paprika*
- ½ tsp ground celery seeds*
- ½ tsp freshly cracked black pepper*
- ½ tsp garlic powder*
- 2¼ tsp fine Himalayan pink salt*
- 1.5 kg pork scotch roast, roughly diced
- 1 fresh bay leaf*
- 700–800 ml Oma's 24-Hour Chicken Broth (see page 55)
- 2–4 tsp cornflour (optional)
- sour cream, to serve

SPICE SHORTCUTS*
2¾ tbsp Gewürzhaus Oma Rosa's Gulasch

Set a large pressure cooker to medium heat, add the oil and sweat the onion until translucent, 8–10 minutes, stirring frequently. Add the spices and salt and stir.

Turn up the heat to medium–high and add the meat. Stir frequently and cook until the pork is sealed, about 8 minutes. Add the bay leaf and enough stock to cover the meat and stir.

Close the pressure cooker after checking the safety valve. Turn up the heat. When the pressure is reached, reduce the heat to low and cook for 25–35 minutes, until the meat is tender and pulls apart easily. Release the steam to bring the pressure down to a safe level before opening the lid. (If you don't have a pressure cooker, you can cook the *Gulasch* in a large saucepan over low heat for 2–3 hours.)

Once cooked, you can thicken the liquid. Do this especially if you are serving the *Gulasch* with dumplings or noodles, as they won't absorb the liquid like potatoes will. In a small bowl, mix the cornflour with just enough water until smooth. Whisk this into the hot *Gulasch* until it has thickened.

Serve with Silesian Potato Dumplings (page 102) or steamed potatoes and sour cream. Store leftovers in an airtight container in the fridge for up to 1 week, or freeze in portions for up to 4 months.

COOK'S NOTES: *If you don't have Hungarian noble sweet paprika, substitute it with Spanish* dulce *paprika. The quality and type of paprika really matters here. Make sure your paprika is vibrant and sweet, and that its fiery red colour permeates the oil.*

OMA ROSA'S GULASCH (PAGE 98) WITH SILESIAN POTATO DUMPLINGS (PAGE 102)

Silesian Potato Dumplings

SCHLESISCHE KARTOFFELKLÖSSE

Our maternal grandmother came from the city of Bytom in Silesia, where these easy-to-make, sauce-retaining dumplings are standard fare. Unlike the more common half-and-half German dumplings, Silesian potato dumplings are made with minimal fuss and only three ingredients. They are sticky and moreish, delicious with a rich gravy, such as the one from Oma Rosa's Gulasch (page 98). Although we never met our grandmother on our mother's side, making these dumplings connects us back to our ancestors and their traditions, and I often wonder how big she rolled her dumplings and what she would say about mine. – ***Maria***

SERVES 4–5

Gluten free / Dairy free / Vegan

- 1 kg large, even-sized Dutch cream potatoes, washed
- 2 tsp cooking salt
- 1–2 cups potato starch, plus extra for dusting
- 1¾ tsp good-quality sea salt, such as fleur de sel

Place the washed potatoes in a large saucepan of cold water with 1 teaspoon of the cooking salt. Bring to a rolling boil and cook for 15–20 minutes, until a fork pierces a potato with little resistance. When ready, drain and set aside to cool.

Peel the potatoes as soon as you can handle them. Grate them into a large, wide bowl using a coarse grater or a potato ricer.

Evenly distribute the grated potato in the bowl, then press it down gently to flatten a little. Mark the surface into four even quadrants, then cut through the potato to the base of the bowl. Scoop out one-quarter of the potato and place it on top of the other potato, leaving one quadrant empty.

Fill the empty quadrant with sifted potato starch up to the height of the rest of the potato to measure out an equal quadrant. Add the sea salt to the bowl, then mix the starch into the grated potato until the starch is more or less absorbed. Turn the dough out onto a floured bench and knead until it comes together into a smooth mass.

Bring a large saucepan of water to the boil and add the remaining teaspoon of cooking salt.

Pinch off chunks of dough and roll them into balls, about the size of a golf ball. Press each ball into a flat disc. Using your thumb, make an even indentation in each disc. Set aside.

Lower the dumplings carefully into the boiling water and cook for 8–10 minutes, until the dumplings are floating on the surface. Turn off the heat and leave the dumplings to steep for 1 minute before draining.

You can store uncooked dumplings in the fridge for a few days, or freeze cooked dumplings for up to 3 months.

Leftover Dumpling Hash with Onion & Bacon

BRATKNÖDEL MIT SPECK UND ZWIEBELN

I daydream about this dish regularly. When I make potato dumplings, I always make a double batch so that there is absolutely no chance that my family can possibly consume all of the dumplings at dinner, leaving none for me to whip up a batch of these crispy and golden, yet pillowy soft dumplings the next day for breakfast or lunch. I usually make these with a few pinches of *Bratkartoffel* spice – Germany's solution to all things fried or baked potatoes. Smoked paprika is equally delicious, as is a pinch of chipotle or some smoked salt. – ***Maria***

SERVES 1–2
Gluten free

6 leftover Silesian Potato Dumplings (page 102)

2 tbsp grapeseed oil

½ onion, halved again and finely sliced

2 bacon rashers, roughly diced

2 garlic cloves, crushed

¼ tsp dried thyme*

sea salt flakes*

freshly cracked black pepper*

a few pinches of smoked paprika*

sour cream, to serve

snipped chives, to serve

SPICE SHORTCUTS*
1 tsp Gewürzhaus Bratkartoffel Spice

Fill a heatproof bowl three-quarters full with boiling water. Carefully place the dumplings in the bowl and reheat for 5 minutes. Drain and cut the dumplings into bite-sized pieces. (You could also reheat them in the microwave.)

Heat the oil in a large frying pan over medium heat. When the oil is hot, add the dumplings. Fry for about 7 minutes, until the dumplings are starting to colour. Add the onion, bacon, garlic and thyme and fry until everything is golden brown, about 6 minutes. Season with salt and pepper and the smoked paprika. Stir and cook for a further minute.

Top with a generous dollop of sour cream, scatter over some chives and serve.

Store any leftovers in an airtight container in the fridge for a day or two.

COOK'S NOTES: *If you want to make this with freshly cooked dumplings, simply omit the first step of reheating and draining the dumplings.*

Gabi's North German Cucumber Salad

GABIS NORDDEUTSCHER GURKENSALAT

Mum made this simple salad a lot when we were kids, and it was one of our favourites. Sweet and tangy and so refreshing, you can eat this on its own or serve it as a side to barbecued meats. I make it in the height of summer when the cucumbers in our veggie garden seem to magically appear overnight. – ***Maria***

SERVES 4 AS A SIDE
Gluten free / Dairy free / Vegan

- 2 continental cucumbers or 3–4 Lebanese cucumbers, ends chopped off and peeled if the skin is tough and bitter
- ¼ onion, finely chopped (optional)
- 1½ tsp fine Himalayan pink salt
- freshly ground black pepper
- 1 tsp dried dill tips (or 2–3 dill sprigs, finely chopped)
- 80 ml (⅓ cup) white vinegar
- 2–3 tsp white sugar

Using a mandoline or sharp knife, finely slice the cucumbers into a mixing bowl. Add the onion (if using). Add the salt and mix it in with your hands, squeezing the cucumber and onion a little as you go. Let the cucumbers sit at room temperature for 15 minutes.

Add the pepper, dill, vinegar and sugar to taste, and mix these into the cucumbers well. You are aiming for a punchy balance of sweet, sour and salty.

The salad will keep in an airtight container in the fridge for up to 1 week.

Cabbage Salad with Coriander & Caraway Oil

KRAUTSALAT MIT KORIANDER-UND KÜMMELÖL

Cabbage has always been a staple in our grandmother's Hungarian-influenced kitchen and in our mother's German kitchen. From a simple *Krautsalat* like this one, to sauerkraut or braised cabbage, it snuck its way into many meals and was a highlight of others as we grew up. I've only really come to appreciate how deliciously sweet and crunchy cabbage can be since growing my own and buying it seasonally from our local farmers' market. Though this is a simple salad, be warned – it's not for the faint-hearted. It's a bit like a shot of strong *Schnaps* – at first sobering from the hit of onion and hard vinegar, then, when you acclimatise and the nuances of the flavours evolve, it's just bloody good and will have you going back for more and more. And also like a good *Schnaps*, it feels digestion-aiding, so is well paired with rich, fatty meats. – ***Maria***

SERVES 4–6 AS A SIDE
Gluten free / Dairy free / Vegan

- 1 small onion, halved and finely sliced
- fine Himalayan pink salt
- ¼ large white cabbage (about 500 g), finely sliced
- 1–2 flat-leaf parsley sprigs, leaves picked and roughly torn
- 100 ml white vinegar
- 100 ml Coriander & Caraway Oil (page 36)
- freshly cracked black pepper

Place the onion in a medium bowl and sprinkle with a few decent pinches of salt. Massage the salt through the onion and set aside for 15 minutes.

In the meantime, place the cabbage in a large bowl and add a few decent pinches of salt. Massage the salt into the cabbage three to five times and set aside.

When the onion has finished resting, taste some; when the salt has taken the edge off the sharp bitterness, add the onion and parsley to the cabbage and toss to combine. Add the vinegar and oil and mix them through the salad. Season with extra salt and pepper to taste.

COOK'S NOTES: *Salting the onion reduces the acrid taste that strong onion can have. Unlike when soaking in water, salting means you don't pour all of the beautiful sweetness of the onion down the drain.*

Classic German Fondue with Broth

KLASSISCHES FLEISCHFONDUE MIT BRÜHE

In Germany in the '70s and '80s, fondue night was a favourite type of dinner party. As children, we loved taking part in the cook-at-the-table event. Once the fondue pot with hot broth was placed on the base with the flame lit, surrounded by accompanying platters, everyone loaded their forks and started cooking. It was a beautiful, interactive and slow way to enjoy food, often going on until midnight. We remember these evenings with great fondness: different generations sitting around a table, sharing food and stories.

This type of fondue differs from the classic Swiss cheese fondue, the French bourguignonne or the chocolate fondue. It is more opulent with its spread and accompaniments and most probably a German 'invention'. Anything falling off a fondue fork and floating in the broth is free for anyone to eat! – ***Eva***

SERVES 6

about 2 litres Oma's 24-Hour Chicken Broth (see page 55)

Beef marinade

500 g beef porterhouse

1 tbsp light soy sauce

1 garlic clove, crushed

½ onion, finely grated

¼ tsp fine Himalayan pink salt

¼ tsp caster sugar

½ tsp gochugaru chilli flakes

⅛ tsp ground ginger

Chicken marinade

500 g chicken thigh fillets

2 tsp sweet paprika

½ tsp ground coriander seeds

¼ tsp ground yellow mustard seeds

¼ tsp garlic powder

¼ tsp dried thyme

½ tsp fine Himalayan pink salt

1 tbsp extra-virgin olive oil

To prepare the meat, cut the beef and chicken into 1.5 cm cubes. In two separate bowls, mix all the ingredients together for each marinade. Add the beef and chicken to the relevant bowls and mix to coat the meat. Cover and refrigerate for at least 2 hours (overnight is better).

Creamy herb dip

250 g (1 cup) sour cream

¼ cup finely chopped gherkin

¼ cup finely chopped French shallot

¼ cup fresh mixed herbs, finely chopped

½ tsp Dijon mustard

½ tsp sea salt flakes

½ tsp dried dill tips

Chipotle mayonnaise

125 g (½ cup) mayonnaise

2 tbsp ketchup

2 tsp whiskey

½ tsp ground chipotle chilli

¼ tsp fine Himalayan pink salt

Curry dip

¾ tsp ground coriander seeds

½ tsp ground cumin seeds

½ tsp ground turmeric

⅛ tsp ground ginger

⅛ tsp garlic powder

⅛ tsp ground cardamom

⅛ tsp ground cinnamon

3 tbsp mayonnaise

3 tbsp sour cream

1 egg, hard-boiled and peeled

¼ tsp fine Himalayan pink salt

1 tsp lemon juice

¼ tsp caster sugar

Vegetables

1½ cups each of chopped broccoli, onion, mushroom, capsicum and zucchini

For the creamy herb dip and chipotle mayonnaise, simply mix all the ingredients together in two separate bowls.

For the curry dip, blend all the ingredients together in a food processor until you have a nice, smooth dip. Decant into a serving bowl.

Refrigerate the dips for at least 1 hour for the flavours to fully develop. These can be prepared the day before.

Place the vegetables in serving bowls or on a platter.

Set the table with the bowls of uncooked meat and vegetables, the dips and any salads. Heat the broth in a fondue pot on the stovetop over high heat until it reaches boiling point. Depending on the size of your fondue pot, add more or less broth to suit. When hot, check for seasoning and adjust to taste. Bring it to the table and place it on the lit fondue base. Now everyone can load their fondue forks with the ingredients and place them into the hot broth to cook.

COOK'S NOTES: *Any protein and most vegetables can be used for this fondue. Not all the meat needs to be marinated – the chicken broth will give flavour while cooking and there are also the delicious dipping sauces. We always make some salads, such as Cabbage Salad with Coriander & Caraway Oil (page 108) and South German Potato Salad (page 126), and place a fresh baguette on the table.*

CLASSIC GERMAN FONDUE WITH BROTH (PAGES 110–11)

STAUB
FONDUE
STAUB

Eva's Favourite Eggs with Mustard & Dill Sauce

EVAS LIEBLINGSSENFEIER MIT DILL

This was my favourite dish as a child. Mum used to make it for me and Maria never understood why I liked it. During war times when there was not much disposable income, this dish was often cooked as the ingredients were cheap and easily accessible. When I asked Mum for the recipe, she'd totally forgotten how to make it and after a few failed attempts, it luckily came back to her. – ***Eva***

SERVES 4

1 kg (about 6 medium) waxy potatoes, such as Dutch cream, kipfler or desiree, peeled and quartered

1 tsp cooking salt

8 eggs

chopped dill fronds, to serve

freshly cracked black pepper

Mustard & dill sauce

100 g salted butter, plus extra to serve

100 g (⅔ cup) plain flour

600 ml full-cream milk

400 ml Oma's 24-Hour Chicken Broth (page 55)

¾ tsp fine Himalayan pink salt

2 tsp white sugar

5 tsp Dijon mustard

2 tsp dried dill tips

Place the potato in a large saucepan of cold water with the cooking salt. Bring to a rolling boil and cook for about 15 minutes or until the potato is still a little firm when pierced with a fork. Strain the potato and melt a little butter over it.

To make the sauce, melt the butter in a saucepan over medium heat, then add the flour and stir until combined. Cook, stirring continuously, for about 3 minutes. Add 125 ml (½ cup) of the milk at a time, whisking until smooth each time. Do the same with the broth. By the end, you will have a beautifully smooth sauce. Whisk in the salt, sugar, mustard and dill, then cook on low heat for 10 minutes, stirring occasionally.

Place the eggs in a medium saucepan, cover with water and bring to a rolling boil over high heat. Turn the heat off and let the eggs stand for 6 minutes, then strain. Place the saucepan under running, cold water until the eggs are just cool enough to handle. Peel each egg after gently cracking the shells all over. You can leave the eggs whole or halve them. Carefully add the eggs to the sauce, turn off the heat, cover and let sit for 5 minutes.

To serve, arrange the potato and eggs on each plate and pour over the sauce. Sprinkle with chopped dill and cracked pepper.

You can store leftovers in an airtight container in the fridge for a few days.

COOK'S NOTES: *Traditional roux recipes heat the milk/stock before adding it to the butter and flour mix. I like to save on washing up, so I add it in cold and just take more time to make sure the mixture is smooth before adding any more.*

German Mac 'n' Cheese

SCHWÄBISCHE KÄSSPÄTZLE MIT RÖSTZWIEBELN

The title says it all, this is a fancy version of mac 'n' cheese with homemade German noodles, crispy onions and gooey cheese. Simple flavours that just work together.

SERVES 4
Vegetarian

450 g (3 cups) plain flour

4 eggs

¼ tsp ground nutmeg

1 tsp fine Himalayan pink salt

300 g cheese, grated (we use a mixture of Gruyère, cheddar and Gouda in equal parts; Emmentaler and Jarlsberg are also excellent options)

Caramelised onion

60 g salted butter

1 large onion, halved and sliced

pinch of fine Himalayan pink salt

pinch of white sugar

First, make the caramelised onion. In a large frying pan, melt the butter over medium heat. Add the onion and fry until golden brown, about 20–30 minutes. Halfway through cooking, add the salt and sugar to help the caramelisation. Set aside.

Preheat the oven to 200°C fan-forced.

Bring a large saucepan of water to the boil over high heat.

To make the *Spätzle* (noodles), place the flour, eggs, nutmeg and salt in a mixing bowl. With a wooden spoon, lightly mix the ingredients together. Gradually add 250 ml (1 cup) of cold water, a little at a time, while stirring, until the dough just comes together. Do not overmix – better less than too much.

Fill a *Spätzle* maker with some of the dough and quickly move the dough box back and forth over the pan of boiling water, so the *Spätzle* fall into the water. Continue until the dough box is empty. Cook for 1–2 minutes, until the *Spätzle* rise to the top. Using a large slotted spoon, take them out of the pan, gently shaking off the excess water, then transfer to an ovenproof dish. Add a layer of cheese and continue until all the *Spätzle* are made and the cheese is used up.

Sprinkle the caramelised onion over the top, then bake in the hot oven for 10 minutes. The cheese will have melted and the corners will start to get nice and crunchy.

COOK'S NOTES: *This recipe calls for a* Spätzle *maker – or, in German,* Spätzlehobel *– to make the noodles. You can find these online by searching 'spaetzle maker'. Alternatively, some European delis sell dried* Spätzle *that you can simply cook to make this recipe. This is a much wetter dough than regular pasta dough, as it needs to be wet to pass through the* Spätzle *maker.*

WHAT'S IN A STITCH?

'It's a remarkable thing to take a piece of fabric, a needle and some thread and to create something beautiful with only time, patience, skill and imagination.'

It might surprise you that embroidery is one of the oldest, continuously practised art forms in human existence. It goes much further back than today's plastic-wrapped DIY kits of puppies and monsteras; much further back even than Jane Austen's Lizzy making satin stitches on her hoop in her sitting room. According to the journal *Antiquity*, the remains of embroidery have been discovered dating as far back as the 5th century BC.

Embroidery has endured and, along the way, it has served as an important medium for conveying and preserving story, myth, fable and religious beliefs in its stitches and symbols. Folk embroidery and weavings travelled via the early traders and so migrated: the library of patterns spreading to wherever humans could go, still informing our stitches today.

Everyday embroidery was largely in the realm of women, skills passing down the line from grandmother to daughter to granddaughter. The many hours, often months or years, required to complete something as elaborate and detailed as a cross-stitch pattern were reserved for those with the patience to see something through that was not immediately gratifying, for those with a love of detail, of creation.

When we were kids, Eva and I would often sit pondering why our grandmother would bother with intricate lacework, so fine that even several hours of work would produce no apparent progress. Why bother with such fiddly work? Why bother doing a cross-stitch pattern to embellish a tablecloth when you could just go to the shops and buy a printed equivalent, the transformation complete within a few hours rather than months. It seemed to us the folly of the old, killing time when there was nothing else to do.

Now, we feel very differently about this.

Something must have stuck with me from watching my grandmother, because I did take up embroidery some years later. I started on a very small cross-stitch kit, an illustration of an Easter bunny. It took me all holidays to complete. My Oma looked on over my shoulder as she worked on her own project, guiding me when I got stuck, few sounds other than the ticking of the noisy clock in her tiny apartment accompanying us in our methodical work. It was my first foray into the art of embroidery, into the many important things that come from completing a project.

It's a remarkable thing to take a piece of fabric, a needle and some thread and to create something beautiful with only time, patience, skill and imagination. In the times before printed patterns, the embroideress would carefully fold her fabric to find the centre and mark it with a little stitched cross. And then she would start, whatever creativity coming out of her flowing through the needle onto the cloth, part imagination, part inspiration.

The start of the project was always the hardest; days needed to pass before a rhythm was established, before she could pick up the piece and start to feel comfortable with the task at hand. Weeks in and the embroideress would be working at a steady pace, starting to fill in sections of her work, starting to feel at one with the piece. Seasons would come and go; she may have started in the depths of winter, sitting by a fire, snow covering everything outside, the colours of the yarn the only brightness she could focus on. Spring, summer, autumn and perhaps winter pass again before the tablecloth she is embroidering is nearing completion. She has worked for a prolonged period of time, many things occurring – perhaps birth and death, a good harvest, a plague. Her many experiences flow into the cloth and make it timeless. When Christmas arrives, she carefully presses the finished work and lays it on the table. She feels a deep sense of peace, knowing that she has endured through all life has thrown her way; she has finished what she started with nothing more than a cross on a piece of plain fabric and some age-old stitches.

This cloth will become one of her most enduring gifts to her family. When she is no longer of this earth, her children will in turn carefully press that cloth and lay it out on Christmas Day, cherishing her memory and feeling her energy renewed in the space they together inhabit.

—

We are blessed to have many precious embroidered tablecloths in our collections, some bought, most handed down, some completed ourselves. We treasure each one, knowing how much attention, love and work has gone into them. On our tables, they help to bring together our families.

– Maria

Semolina Dumpling Soup

GRIEẞKLÖẞCHENSUPPE

These days, this is my favourite dish, and when you exclude ice cream, it's my daughters' favourite dish also, or at least on par with pizza! We make it often, especially in the colder months of the year. They affectionately refer to the soup dumplings as *Wolken*, translating to clouds. – ***Eva***

SERVES 6
Dairy free

4 litres Oma's 24-Hour Chicken Broth (page 55)

3 carrots, cut into 1 cm rounds

Dumplings

2 eggs, separated

fine Himalayan pink salt

100–120 g coarse semolina

pinch of ground nutmeg

pinch of ground cinnamon

Heat the broth in a large saucepan to a rapid simmer. Add the carrots and cook until soft, about 15 minutes. Season to taste.

When the carrots are almost cooked through, start making the dumplings. In a bowl, using electric beaters, beat the egg whites with a pinch of salt until stiff peaks form. Add the semolina and spices and gently fold them through until combined. Add the egg yolks and fold them in. Try to leave as much air in the egg white mixture as possible.

Using two spoons, make quenelles with the mixture and gently drop them into the low-simmering broth. Cook for 2 minutes, then turn off the heat and let the dumplings steep in the broth, with the lid on, for a further 5 minutes.

Store any leftovers in an airtight container in the fridge for a few days.

Speckled Late Summer Vegetables

GEFLECKTES SPÄTSOMMER GEMÜSE

Black limes, smoked paprika, nigella and poppy seeds, Aleppo pepper – this is a list of wild and big-flavoured spices. When they come together, with olive oil and garlic and the juices of late summer vegetables, they sing in chorus and create a beautiful dish that is enjoyable with every bite. Serve them just like this – they don't need anything else. – ***Maria***

SERVES 4–5
Gluten free / Dairy free / Vegetarian

extra-virgin olive oil, for drizzling

600 g kipfler or Dutch cream potatoes, cut lengthways into thin wedges

500 g (2 small) eggplant, cut lengthways into thin wedges

½ red capsicum, deseeded and sliced

2 tomatoes, cut into wedges

3 red onions, cut into wedges

Black lime & nigella spice blend

1½ tsp black lime powder made from 2–3 black limes (see method)

1 tbsp plus 1 tsp smoked sea salt flakes

1 tbsp nigella seeds

1 tbsp blue poppy seeds

2 tsp Aleppo pepper

¾ tsp smoked paprika

Aïoli

10 garlic cloves, unpeeled and cut in half

160 g (⅔ cup) whole-egg mayonnaise

Preheat the oven to 200°C fan-forced.

Roughly crush the black limes. Place in a food processor and process until as fine as possible. Transfer to a jar and label what you don't use in this recipe.

To make the spice blend, combine all the ingredients in a bowl. Mix and set aside.

Coat a large (41 cm × 32 cm) sheet pan in oil. Add the potato and eggplant. Douse them in oil on all sides, then spread them out evenly, sitting all the wedges on their skins. Sprinkle three-quarters of the spice mix over the vegetables, making sure they are well coated in the spices on all sides. Add the garlic for the aïoli to one part of the pan (as you need to remove these later) and drizzle with oil. Bake in the oven for 20 minutes.

In the meantime, place the capsicum, tomato and onion in a large bowl. Drizzle them very generously with oil, tossing as you go. Add the remaining spice blend and mix it through well.

After the potato and eggplant have been baking for 20 minutes, briefly remove the sheet pan from the oven. Reduce the heat to 180°C fan-forced. Remove the garlic and set aside. Add the vegetables from the bowl to the pan, mixing them through the potato and eggplant carefully. Return to the oven for a further 20 minutes.

To make the aïoli, squeeze the garlic pulp out of the skins into a small bowl. Squash the pulp to a paste with a fork – there should be clumps of garlic. Add the mayonnaise and stir well.

When the vegetables are cooked, arrange them on large plates and serve with a dollop of aïoli on the side.

The vegetables will keep in an airtight container in the fridge for up to 1 week. The aïoli will keep for 2 weeks in a small sealed jar in the fridge.

South German Potato Salad

SCHWÄBISCHER KARTOFFELSALAT

We grew up in the south of Germany, in a little town called Hürben, with a population of just under 1000! Here the potato salad is made with a mixture of vinegar, stock and oil, not like in the north, where they add mayonnaise, a true crime if you ask a *Schwabe*. Each year, the town hosts the *Hürbener Dorffest*, the town festival where our family friend Helga leads the charge in making 125 kilos of potato salad, and her husband Friedel heads up the Roll-Me-Home Brothers, the local band with a fitting name. – ***Eva***

SERVES 4
Dairy free / Vegan

- 1 kg firm, waxy potatoes, such as desiree, of even size
- ½ large white onion, very finely chopped
- 250 ml (1 cup) chicken, beef or vegetable stock (or use Oma's 24-Hour Chicken Broth, page 55)
- 1½ tbsp malt vinegar
- 2 tbsp white wine vinegar
- 1½ tbsp apple cider vinegar
- 1½ tsp fine Himalayan pink salt
- ½ tsp crushed celery seeds
- 3 tbsp sunflower oil

Leaving the skin on, wash the potatoes and place them in a large pot. Add water until it is only half covering the potatoes. This lets them cook/steam without bouncing around so much. With the lid on, bring to a simmer and cook for 20–30 minutes. Test the potatoes with the point of a knife or skewer – they should be firm but not raw in the middle.

Drain the potatoes and set them aside to cool slightly. While still warm, peel and cut them in half, then cut them into about 5 mm thick slices. Place the potato in a bowl and gently mix with the onion.

Heat the stock, vinegars, salt and celery seeds in a small saucepan over medium heat until warm, then pour the mixture over the still-warm potato. Set aside for 10 minutes for the potato to absorb the liquid. Carefully mix the oil into the potato and let it infuse for at least 1 hour prior to serving.

This salad is best made the day before. Remove it from the fridge to allow it to come to room temperature before serving.

COOK'S NOTES: *In Germany, there is a specific vinegar called* Hengstenberg Altmeister Essig, *which is traditionally used for this recipe. You can order it online, or some German or Polish delis stock it. We have done our best to recreate it using more conventional vinegars but, if you can source it, use it in place of the malt, white wine and apple cider vinegars.*

Moroccan Apricot Chicken Traybake

MAROKKANISCHES APRIKOSENHUHN VOM BLECH

This traybake is so easy to throw together on a weeknight and is a hit with my kids. You could even prep this the day before, then just place it in the oven after work. My husband and I love the bonus accompaniment – whiskey sours made with the aquafaba from the canned chickpeas. – ***Maria***

SERVES 4
Gluten free

- 10 strands of saffron
- 400 g can chickpeas
- 500 g chicken thigh fillets
- 600 g butternut pumpkin
- zest of 1 orange
- juice of 2 oranges
- 5 parsley sprigs, chopped
- 135 g (¾ cup) dried apricots
- 1 tsp ground cumin*
- 1 tsp ground coriander seeds*
- ¼ tsp ground cardamom seeds*
- ¼ tsp cayenne pepper*
- ½ tsp ground ginger*
- 1 tsp dried thyme
- 1 tbsp salted capers
- 3 tbsp red wine vinegar
- 3 tbsp extra-virgin olive oil
- 3 tbsp honey
- 2 dried bay leaves
- 1 garlic bulb, cut in half
- 1 onion, cut into 6 wedges
- Greek-style yoghurt, to serve

SPICE SHORTCUTS*
3 tsp Gewürzhaus Moroccan Souk Spice

Preheat the oven to 160°C fan-forced.

Soften the saffron in a teaspoon of hot water for 10 minutes.

Drain the chickpeas, reserving the liquid to make whiskey sours (see recipe below). Set aside.

Cut the chicken into large chunks. Peel the pumpkin and cut it into 2 cm cubes. Set aside.

In a very large baking tray, combine the orange zest, orange juice, parsley (reserve some as a garnish), apricots, saffron with water, spices, thyme, capers, vinegar, oil and honey. Mix everything together well. Add the bay leaves, garlic, onion, chicken, pumpkin and chickpeas. Mix again so that all the ingredients are coated in the marinade.

Bake for 20 minutes. Turn the chicken and vegetables and bake for a further 20 minutes until the vegetables are cooked through and golden. Season to taste and serve with yoghurt and the reserved parsley scattered over the top.

Store any leftovers in an airtight container in the fridge for several days, or freeze for up to 4 months.

COOK'S NOTES: *We use unsulphured Turkish dried apricots in this recipe.*

—

Maple & Nutmeg Whiskey Sour

Place 60 ml of high-quality bourbon, 30 ml of lemon juice, 10–15 ml of maple syrup and 20 ml of the reserved chickpea liquid (aquafaba) in a cocktail mixer and shake. Add a few ice cubes and shake vigorously. Pour into a whiskey glass full of ice. Grate some nutmeg on top to garnish.

Creamy Veal & Wild Mushroom Stew

RAHMGESCHNETZELTES MIT PILZEN

When writing for this book, some recipes had many iterations. Mum helped me with this one; it came together harmoniously and we look forward to cooking it for many mushrooming seasons to come. – ***Eva***

SERVES 4

- 500 g veal schnitzels
- 3 tbsp plain flour
- 60 g salted butter, plus 30 g extra
- 2 tbsp extra-virgin olive oil
- 1 onion, quartered and sliced
- 300 g saffron milk cap mushrooms, sliced
- 125 ml (½ cup) white wine
- 250 ml (1 cup) thickened cream
- 375 ml (1½ cups) chicken stock
- 1½ tsp Dijon mustard
- ¾ tsp fine Himalayan pink salt
- 2 tsp lemon juice
- 1 tbsp chopped flat-leaf parsley

Spice mixture

- 1 tsp ground coriander seeds
- ¾ tsp fine Himalayan pink salt
- ¾ tsp ground cumin seeds
- ¾ tsp dried marjoram
- ¾ tsp garlic powder
- ½ tsp porcini powder
- ½ tsp ground yellow mustard seeds
- ½ tsp dried thyme
- ½ tsp sweet paprika
- ¼ tsp ground mace

To make the spice mixture, mix all the ingredients together.

To prepare the veal, pat it dry, remove the sinew and cut the veal into 1 cm x 5 cm strips. Place the veal, 1 tablespoon of the spice mixture and the flour into a large ziplock bag and mix until the veal is coated. If the meat is sticking together, add a little more flour.

In a large frying pan, heat half the butter and half the oil. Fry the veal over high heat in small batches until browned. Add more butter/oil as needed. Remove the veal from the pan and set aside. Add the onion and mushroom to the pan and sauté over medium heat for 5 minutes – you may need a little more oil. Add the white wine and stir to deglaze the pan. Continue cooking until it has almost evaporated.

In a bowl, whisk together the cream, stock, remaining spice mixture, mustard, salt and lemon juice until smooth. Add this and the veal to the mushrooms in the pan and cook for approximately 5 minutes, stirring occasionally. The flour from the veal coating will thicken the sauce. If it is still too runny, mix 1 tablespoon of cornflour with a little cold water and add a little at a time, stirring it through the mixture until the desired consistency is reached.

Remove from the heat, then add the extra butter and the parsley. Mix through until the butter has melted. Serve straight away with mashed potatoes or pasta.

COOK'S NOTES: *This recipe calls for freshly foraged saffron milk cap mushrooms, also known as pine mushrooms. Swiss browns or champignons will work well, too. You can easily make this gluten free by using gluten-free flour.*

THE MOTHER'S DAY MUSHROOM HUNT

'She has taught us how to identify a slippery jack and a saffron milk cap, as well as other mushrooms in mixed forests or pastures further afield. Without her, we probably wouldn't be here on Mother's Day, collecting mushrooms.'

It's our family tradition to go mushrooming on Mother's Day. It's one of the things we look forward to the most in autumn – packing up beanies and boots and kids and snacks, and heading to the forest. We drive out to our favourite spot, unload baskets and mushroom knives and camping chairs and picnics, car doors opening and closing en masse. We are rugged up and greet each other with padded hugs.

The kids run off, eager to resume the games they made up last year, right here in the same forest. We hear their cooees and chatter fading into the distance. The adults pour cups of coffee and tea out of thermoses. It's markedly colder than in the city and even in the nearby town, the shade of the pine trees dropping the thermostat by several clicks, and so we warm up on stories and the hot brew in our cold hands in the midst of the forest. Our dad is always straight off with a big basket, the mission of filling it with mushrooms calling him more strongly than anyone else.

Eventually, we are all walking among the pines, heads down, eyes peeled, looking for fungal treasure. Mushrooming is a bit like puzzling – in time, your eyes become trained to find what you are searching for. A bulge in the fallen needles, a lone mushroom in a light well – these are signs to look more closely. There is the occasional call of 'Oma!'/'Mum!'/'Gabi!', as someone requires the expert identification assistance of our mother, the chief mushroomer. In the forest, she is the matriarch and demi-mushroom-goddess, her understanding of the fungus revered and respected. She has taught us how to identify a slippery jack and a saffron milk cap, as well as other mushrooms in mixed forests or pastures further afield. Without her, we probably wouldn't be here on Mother's Day, collecting mushrooms. Because who would have taught us? It's a beautiful thing to celebrate her as a mother, out here in the forest. To see her in her element reminds us of all that she has given us and taught us.

Eventually, we head back towards the cars and chairs and picnics, baskets filled with our hauls. Most years, we start a fire and roast chestnuts. A big cast-iron pan gets heated and we sauté onion and garlic in really good butter. A few people will sit and clean off a mix of mushrooms for the pan, brushing them gently with one of the little mushroom brushes floating around. There's easy chatter as we are busy with tasks, the fresh, crisp air and the simple, uncluttered surrounds putting us at ease, slowing our minds.

Pilze
Einfach sicher Pilze sammeln
andbuch für Pilzsammler

When the mushrooms, thyme and parsley hit the pan, our bellies begin to rumble, switched on by the heavenly wafts joining the smells of the forest. Someone cuts generous slices of fresh and crusty sourdough, slathering them in butter, ready to be used as edible plates for our mushroom fry-up. On it goes, topped with a sprinkle of fleur de sel or another really good, clean salt. Never do the mushrooms taste as good as they do then.

Later in the day, when the kids are exhausted and the thermoses have run dry, we take the remaining harvest home to cook a pot of risotto or pasta or soup. What we don't use for dinner, we dry. Some of us do this in a very low oven or a dehydrator. Others cut the mushrooms into pieces and string them up on lengths of thread to hang in a window, just like Mum did as a young woman after trips to her favourite mushroom hunting grounds in Germany. When the mushrooms are dry, we place them in a jar, or pulverise them in a food processor. They feed us in all of the months when we can't gather them freshly, the aromatics and taste they add taking us straight back to the forest. We look forward to the next year, when we will all meet again to share in this simple ritual as a family.

Forest Mushroom Fry-Up

PILZEPFANNE

When we go mushroom foraging in the pine forest, we often do a cook-up there, either directly on the fire, or on a camping stove. This recipe has been written to cook at home; when we make it in the outdoors, we omit the pasta and serve the fried mushrooms on crusty sourdough bread. It's simple, warm and tasty.

SERVES 4
Vegetarian

- 500 g dried pasta
- 100 g salted butter
- 2 tbsp extra-virgin olive oil
- 6 garlic cloves, crushed
- 600 g foraged edible mushrooms, cleaned and sliced
- 120 ml white wine
- 2 tsp dried thyme
- 1 tsp dried parsley
- 1 tsp sweet paprika
- ¾ tsp fine Himalayan pink salt
- 1½ tbsp lemon juice
- freshly grated pecorino, to serve

Heat a large pot of salted water and cook the pasta according to the packet instructions.

In the meantime, over medium–high heat, melt 60 g of the butter with the oil in a frying pan. Once it starts to become foamy, add the garlic and mushroom. Cook for about 5 minutes, stirring occasionally, before adding the white wine, herbs, paprika, salt and lemon juice. Reduce the heat to a simmer and cook for about 10–15 minutes until soft. Depending on how much moisture is in the mushrooms, you may need to add a little water.

Drain the pasta, reserving 100 ml of the cooking water. Add the cooked pasta to the frying pan as well as the reserved cooking water and toss. Add the remaining butter and toss until melted through.

Adjust the seasoning and serve with a generous amount of freshly grated pecorino.

COOK'S NOTES: *A mixture of forest mushrooms is perfect, although if using slippery jacks, only add a small quantity of these. We forage mainly saffron milk caps (pine mushrooms). Champignons, portobellos and Swiss browns are all good substitutes.*

SAFFRON
NUTMEG
PARSLEY
LOVAGE
SUMMER SAVOURY

Saffron Minestrone

SAFFRAN GEMÜSEEINTOPF

Saffron is one of my favourite spices to cook with. I love the depth of flavour it gives a dish and how much impact such a little amount of it has. Out of my repertoire of cooking, this is one of those dishes that I often get asked to share the recipe for. It is healthy, easy to make and absolutely delicious. – ***Eva***

SERVES 6

- 250 g speck or pancetta
- 50 g salted butter
- 2½ tbsp extra-virgin olive oil
- 2 celery stalks, chopped into 1 cm pieces
- 2 carrots, halved lengthways, then cut into 2 cm pieces
- 2 small onions, finely chopped
- 3 garlic cloves, crushed
- ½ tsp ground nutmeg
- 15 strands of saffron
- 1 tsp porcini powder
- 1 tsp dried parsley*
- 1 tsp dried lovage*
- 1 tsp dried summer savoury*
- 400 g can crushed tomatoes
- 400 g can mixed beans, drained
- 2 litres Oma's 24-Hour Chicken Broth (page 55)
- 3 tbsp white vinegar
- 350 g pumpkin, chopped into 2 cm cubes (about 2 cups)
- 120 g green beans, chopped into thirds (about 1 cup)
- 160 g (1½ cups) dried orecchiette
- grated parmesan, to serve

Remove the rind from the speck or pancetta and set aside. Chop the speck or pancetta into 1 cm pieces.

In a heavy-based saucepan over medium–low heat, heat the butter and oil. Add the speck or pancetta, rind, celery, carrot, onion, garlic, spices and herbs, and sauté for approximately 30 minutes.

Add the tomatoes, mixed beans, broth and vinegar to the pan and cook on a low simmer for 1 hour. Add the pumpkin and green beans and cook for a further 20 minutes.

Cook the pasta separately in salted water as per the packet instructions. Cooking it in another pan avoids the soup going stodgy – if I have made a big batch of soup to last for a few meals, I cook fresh pasta each time.

Add the cooked pasta to the soup and serve with freshly grated parmesan.

Store any leftovers in an airtight container in the fridge for up to 1 week or freeze for up to 6 months (without the pasta).

COOK'S NOTES: *Lovage is an aromatic herb grown widely in Europe for the peppery, spicy contrast it brings to soups, stocks and vegetables. From the same family as celery, carrot and parsley, lovage is an easy-to-grow perennial that you can pick all summer and dry for the winter.*

SPICE SHORTCUTS*

3 tsp Gewürzhaus Winter Soup Mix

PORCINI
LOVAGE
THYME
ALLSPICE
NUTMEG

Beef Roulades

RINDSROULADEN

This is one of my father's favourite meals. The sauce is the hero of the dish and I smother the roulades and *Spätzle* in it when serving. I really need to remember to make it for him again on our next ski trip. – ***Eva***

SERVES 6–8
Gluten free

- 8 pieces of beef topside
- 8 tbsp Dijon mustard
- sea salt flakes
- freshly cracked black pepper
- 1 onion, finely diced
- 250 g fatty speck, finely diced
- 250 g dill gherkins, finely diced
- extra-virgin olive oil, for frying
- 1 celery stalk, coarsely chopped
- 1 carrot, coarsely chopped
- 1 leek, coarsely chopped
- 1 onion, coarsely chopped
- 1 tsp dried lovage
- 1 tsp dried thyme
- 1 tsp porcini powder
- 1 tsp ground coriander seeds
- ½ tsp celery seeds
- ½ tsp ground allspice
- ½ tsp ground nutmeg
- 70 g tomato paste
- 350 ml red wine (pinot noir or a lighter red is best)
- 500 ml (2 cups) beef stock
- 80 g salted butter, cubed and put into the freezer

Ask your butcher to cut the beef across the grain – each piece should be about 25 cm long, 15 cm wide and 5–7 mm thick.

Pat the beef dry and lay the pieces out, side by side (short sides facing you). Spread 1 tablespoon of mustard onto each piece, then lightly season with salt and pepper.

Mix the onion, speck and gherkin in a bowl and evenly divide the mixture between each piece of meat. Spread the mixture over the meat, leaving a three-finger-wide gap at the short edge furthest away from you, and a one-finger-wide gap along both long edges. Start rolling from the short edge closest to you. Gently fold in the long edges as you tightly roll to the end with the gap. Secure the seam and both sides as best you can with toothpicks or tie them with kitchen string. Repeat until all the roulades are rolled.

On the stove, heat 60–100 ml of oil in a heavy-based oven- and flame-proof casserole or baking dish over high heat and sear the roulades on all sides. Remove from the dish and set aside.

Preheat the oven to 160°C fan-forced.

Add a couple more tablespoons of oil to the dish and sauté the celery, carrot, leek, onion, 1 teaspoon of salt, and the herbs and spices for 5 minutes over medium heat on the stove, stirring regularly. Add the tomato paste and sauté for a further 2 minutes. Deglaze with the wine. Return the roulades to the dish and add enough stock until the roulades are almost covered. With the lid on, cook in the oven for 2 hours.

Remove from the oven and place the roulades in a bowl, covering them to keep them warm. Strain the sauce through a sieve. (You can also blitz the sauce and vegetables for a thicker consistency if you prefer.) Add the cold butter cubes and melt them into the sauce – this will thicken the sauce and make it glossy. Taste and adjust the seasoning.

Place the roulades and sauce back into the dish and serve. These pair well with red cabbage, Silesian Potato Dumplings (page 102), mashed potatoes or *Spätzle* (page 116).

PICTURED ON PAGES 144–5 >

BEEF ROULADES (PAGE 142)

Panko Fish Fingers with Immunity Spices

GESUNDE FISCHSTÄBCHEN

We grew up eating fish fingers and now I just always feel they could have more nutritional value. In developing this recipe, I set out to create a healthy 'TV dinner' that both the kids and I were happy with. The end result is most definitely worth the effort; the fish stays beautifully moist and the coating is crunchy and flavoursome. – ***Eva***

SERVES 4

500 g firm, thick white fish fillets

½ tsp ground turmeric*

¼ tsp garlic powder*

¼ tsp onion powder*

¼ tsp ground ginger*

⅛ tsp ground cloves*

2 tbsp extra-virgin olive oil

Panko crumb

3 tbsp extra-virgin olive oil

90 g (1½ cups) panko breadcrumbs

1 tsp sea salt flakes

2 tsp sweet paprika

3 tbsp freshly grated pecorino

1 tbsp nutritional yeast

Batter

1 egg

2 heaped tbsp whole-egg mayonnaise

2 heaped tbsp plain flour

2 tbsp thickened cream

SPICE SHORTCUTS*
1½ tsp Gewürzhaus Immunity Blend

Pin-bone the fish fillets and remove the skin. Cut the fish into 8 cm × 3 cm pieces and place in a bowl. Add the spices and oil and toss to coat well. Refrigerate for at least 30 minutes.

Preheat the oven to 180°C fan-forced.

For the panko crumb, in a bowl, drizzle the oil over the breadcrumbs and mix in the salt and paprika. Toss to coat the breadcrumbs as evenly as possible. Spread them on a baking tray and bake for 5 minutes or until golden. Set aside. When cool, add the pecorino and nutritional yeast and mix to combine. Transfer to a large plate and set aside.

Turn the oven up to 200°C fan-forced.

Mix all the batter ingredients in a bowl and whisk until they are smooth.

To batter the fish, carefully dip each piece into the batter, then in the breadcrumbs, coating it evenly all over (dip with one hand and crumb with the other!). Place the fish on a lined baking tray. Bake for 15 minutes or until golden brown.

Serve with sautéed carrots and mashed potatoes. Store leftovers in an airtight container in the fridge for several days.

COOK'S NOTES: *This dish includes a range of mild and subtle immune-boosting spices to stay healthy; turmeric helps with the absorption of calcium and cloves are known for their antibacterial properties.*

Mum's Sweet & Sour Bean Soup

MAMAS SÜSS-SAURE BOHNENSUPPE

I have memories of Mum sitting in front of the TV preparing beans for this soup when we were teenagers. She would use a little bean-slicing gadget to cut each bean in strips after she had taken the ends off, *Judge Judy* or *Dr Phil* lightly entertaining her in the process. It was one of our favourite soups with its surprisingly punchy combination of sweet, sour and saltiness, and it's also now a favourite of my kids. They don't like beans, apparently, but that is completely forgotten when this soup is served and they eat like hungry pirates. – ***Maria***

SERVES 6
Gluten free / Dairy free

- extra-virgin olive oil
- 200 g speck, rind removed and reserved, finely diced
- 1 large onion, finely diced
- 7 Dutch cream, nicola or desiree potatoes, peeled and diced into 1 cm cubes
- 2.5 litres Oma's 24-Hour Chicken Broth (page 55)
- 1 kg green beans, trimmed, cut diagonally into 2 cm segments
- 2½ tsp dried summer savoury
- ¼ tsp freshly cracked black pepper
- 2 tbsp sea salt flakes

To season

- 3 tbsp white vinegar
- 2 tbsp white sugar
- ¼ tsp freshly cracked black pepper
- sea salt flakes

Cover the base of a 6 litre pot with oil and place over medium–low heat. Add the speck and fry for about 5 minutes. Add the onion, reduce the heat to low and sweat until translucent, stirring regularly, about 5 minutes. Add the potato, cook briefly, then increase the heat to high and deglaze the pot with the stock. Put a lid on the pot, bring to a simmer, reduce the heat to low and cook for about 20 minutes.

Add the beans, summer savoury and pepper. Season to taste with the salt flakes. Add the speck rind, then stir and bring to a simmer. Cook over low heat for 30 minutes, covered. When the potato is soft, turn the heat off and use a potato masher to carefully mash the potato just a little – maybe 15 times – so you have some mashed and some chunks. This thickens the soup a bit.

Let the soup cool for 15 minutes, then remove and discard the speck rind.

Taste the soup. Now start to season by adding a little of the vinegar, sugar, pepper and salt. You are looking for a punchy broth that is sweet, sour and salty. Add more vinegar, sugar, pepper or salt, as needed.

COOK'S NOTES: *Don't be tempted to leave out the sugar or swap the white vinegar for a more mellow one – this soup needs the sharp aspects of both of these ingredients. If you don't have speck, use a fatty bacon or pork belly instead. Summer savoury, known as* Bohnenkraut *(bean herb) in German, is the perfect partner to green beans and the secret weapon of this soup. The herb is most similar to thyme (but please don't swap it out!).*

A LABOUR OF LOVE

'Somewhere in between the midwives doing their checks and us taking our little bundle to bed, my sister-in-law handed out big plates of warmed-up lasagne and slices of banana bread.'

It happened quite organically that lasagne became a significant part of the night I gave birth to our second child, our daughter, Matilda.

Weeks earlier, I had prepared two big trays of lasagne, both destined for the freezer, ready to be pulled out and stuck in the oven when the time came that our little family went from three to four. I started with the ragu, shaping the mince into large meatballs to fry off, so that I wouldn't have to fiddle around scooping out mince, or lifting the heavy pressure cooker over my belly. Next, sautéing vegetables, including zucchini, which would be carefully hidden in the meaty sauce, my son none the wiser. The aromatics of onion, garlic, carrot and celery filled the house. Next, I fried off tomato paste and spices – oregano, clove, sweet paprika and mushroom powder from last autumn. Deglazed with balsamic vinegar and white wine. A few big, fresh, meaty tomatoes from the garden, some bay leaves from my growing tree and basil, of course. I seasoned, turned the pressure cooker on, and collapsed on the sofa. That was enough for one pregnant day.

The next day, I made the béchamel in my Thermomix (saved from the heat of the stove!), then assembled the lasagne in two large trays. Ragu, lasagne sheets, béchamel, mozzarella. Repeat twice, finishing with béchamel and more mozzarella. Done. I set them aside to cool, covered them in beeswax wraps and put them in the freezer. Now the little tyke could arrive. I was ready.

But she had other plans. Almost two weeks past my due date, she decided it was finally time and arrived in record speed, all the calm-birth breathing and plans of a peaceful birth replaced by a howling labour, as intense as the huge full moon hanging in the midnight sky.

The midwives arrived in time, shortly after my sister-in-law and, before I knew it, Matilda was safely in our arms, her little face precious and perfect, the toil and pain of the last few hours forgotten. We could all breathe out now.

Somewhere in between the midwives doing their checks and us taking our little bundle to bed, my sister-in-law handed out big plates of warmed-up lasagne and slices of banana bread, and we sat around in our living room, eating and reflecting on the last few hours, Matilda in our midst.

On reflection, the importance of sharing this food as a sort of finale really struck me. It's something that doesn't happen in our modern system of hospital births – that those who help you on your journey can sit with you to share a meal you cooked for them. And no ordinary meal; lasagne is a labour of love. Just as birth is a labour of love.

Every year, on Matilda's birthday, I make two big trays of lasagne and whoever in our family is around is welcome to share dinner with us, to celebrate the night our daughter arrived. Food and flavour can transport us to a place in our past in an instant. Lasagne will always be, for me, the food of Matilda. And it is my sincere hope that it, too, will connect her in years to come to the time and place she came from.

– *Maria*

Life-Giving Lasagne

LEBENSSPENDENDE LASAGNE

This recipe makes two big trays of lasagne, because if you are going to go to the effort of making lasagne, you may as well make two. Bake one straight away and put the other one in the freezer. Each tray lasts my family for two meals with a salad, so we get four meals out of this recipe. – ***Maria***

SERVES 12–14

- extra-virgin olive oil
- 500 g pork mince
- 500 g beef mince
- 1 large brown onion, diced
- 1 large red onion, diced
- 4 garlic cloves, crushed
- 3 carrots, grated or finely diced
- 1 small zucchini, grated or finely diced
- 1 celery stalk, finely diced
- fine Himalayan pink salt
- 140 g tomato paste
- 1 tbsp brown sugar
- 2 tbsp sweet paprika
- ⅛ tsp ground cloves
- 1 tsp dried mushroom powder
- 1 tbsp dried oregano
- 3 tbsp balsamic vinegar
- 180 ml (¾ cup) white wine
- 1.2 kg fresh or canned tomatoes, diced
- 3 fresh bay leaves, scrunched up
- 3 basil sprigs, leaves picked and roughly torn
- freshly cracked black pepper

Start by making the pork and beef ragu. Add enough oil to cover the base of an 8 litre pressure cooker. Make four large meatballs out of each batch of mince – this makes the frying process easier.

Place the pressure cooker over medium heat, then add the meatballs – they have to sizzle vigorously on impact with the oil, otherwise they will stick to the pan. Turn after about 5 minutes. Sear on all sides, about 10 minutes. Transfer to a large plate and set aside.

Add the onions, garlic, carrot, zucchini, celery and a few pinches of salt to the pressure cooker and stir to combine. Reduce the heat to medium–low and sauté for 10–15 minutes, stirring regularly, adding more oil if needed. Add the tomato paste, sugar, spices, mushroom powder, oregano and 1½ tablespoons of salt and simmer for 3–5 minutes, stirring regularly, or until the sauce is bubbling.

Turn up the heat slightly, then deglaze the pressure cooker with the vinegar and wine. Add the browned meatballs and break them up using a potato masher. Stir and cook until sticky and caramelised, about 6–8 minutes. Add the tomatoes, mash the sauce again thoroughly and cook for 2 minutes. Add 1.2 litres of hot water, then stir in the bay leaves and basil. Season with salt and pepper to taste. Close the pressure cooker after checking the safety valve and increase the temperature to high. When the pressure is reached, reduce the heat to low and cook for 20 minutes. Release the steam to bring the pressure down to a safe level before opening the lid.

Béchamel

1.4 litres full-cream milk

1 fresh bay leaf

pinch of ground nutmeg

pinch of cayenne pepper

pinch of ground white pepper

110 g salted butter

110 g (¾ cup) plain flour

1¼ tsp fine Himalayan pink salt

40 g Parmigiano Reggiano or Grana Padano, grated

To assemble

2 × 280 g packets of fresh lasagne sheets

400 g mozzarella ball, grated

To make the béchamel, gently warm the milk in a saucepan over low heat with the bay leaf, nutmeg, cayenne and white pepper.

In a separate medium to large pot – preferably copper or heavy-based – melt the butter over medium–low heat. Add the flour and stir until well combined. Let the mixture cook, stirring regularly, for 1–2 minutes. When the mixture is bubbling up like a pancake and starting to dry out a little, remove from the heat. You want a light roux so this whole process should only take a few minutes from when the flour goes in to when you take the pot off the heat.

Remove the bay leaf from the milk and place in the compost. Add a couple of ladlefuls of milk to the flour mixture and whisk vigorously to fully blend it in. When the mixture is thickened and smooth, slowly add the remaining milk and whisk. If it starts to clump or feels too dry, add more milk and keep stirring. Add the salt and cheese. Return to the heat and cook until the sauce is thickened and the flour taste is gone, stirring continuously, about 5–10 minutes. Remove and set aside.

Preheat the oven to 180°C fan-forced. Butter two large baking dishes, about 33 cm × 26 cm.

To assemble, start by adding three ladlefuls of the ragu to each dish and spread it over the base evenly. Add a single layer of lasagne sheets and press down slightly so they are touching the sauce. If they are curling up, add 1–2 tablespoons of boiling water. Add a layer of béchamel to fully cover the lasagne sheets, then add a layer of mozzarella. Repeat this full process two more times. On top of the third layer of pasta sheets, add a thick layer of béchamel and finish with a layer of mozzarella.

Bake for 35–45 minutes. Rest for 15 minutes before serving.

Store any leftovers in an airtight container in the fridge for up to 1 week.

COOK'S NOTES: *San Marzano or Roma tomatoes are best for making the ragu. Using a pressure cooker for this recipe speeds the process up dramatically and the flavour is ace. If you don't have a pressure cooker, make this in a large heavy-based pot and increase the water somewhat to allow for the extra evaporation. Simmer for 1–2 hours, until the sauce has thickened slightly.*

Fish Pie with Mashed Celeriac Crust

FISCHAUFLAUF MIT KNOLLENSELLERIE PÜREE

I especially like the texture in this pie: the chunky fish, the smooth mash with its crusty top and the softness of the leek. It is mild in flavour yet quite complex, with the saffron giving it depth and balance. – ***Eva***

SERVES 6
Gluten free

- 800 g firm white fish fillets
- 500 g floury potatoes
- 500 g celeriac
- 1 dried bay leaf
- 200 ml full-cream milk
- 300 ml fish stock
- 2 garlic cloves, crushed
- 1 leek, white part only, sliced
- 2 tbsp extra-virgin olive oil
- 3 tbsp white wine
- 155 g (1 cup) frozen peas
- juice of ½ lemon
- generous pinch of saffron
- 80 g salted butter
- freshly grated pecorino, to serve

Spice paste

- 1 tsp ground fennel seeds*
- 1 tsp ground yellow mustard seeds*
- 1 tsp dried dill tips*
- ½ tsp ground turmeric*
- ½ tsp ground nutmeg*
- ¼ tsp ground allspice*
- ¼ tsp ground ginger*
- 2 tbsp extra-virgin olive oil

Preheat the oven to 200°C fan-forced.

Pin-bone and skin the fish, then cut it into large chunks. Place in a medium bowl, add all the spice paste ingredients and mix well. Refrigerate until needed.

Peel and dice the potatoes and celeriac. Bring a saucepan of salted water to the boil and cook the potato and celeriac until soft, about 15–20 minutes.

In the meantime, place the fish, bay leaf, milk and stock in a saucepan over medium heat and bring to a low boil. Reduce to a low simmer and cook for 8 minutes with the lid on. Strain the liquid off and reserve it. Place the bay leaf in the compost. Break the fish into large flakes and spread it into a 22 cm round baking dish.

Fry the garlic and leek in the oil in a saucepan over medium heat for 5 minutes, or until soft. Deglaze the pan with the wine. Set aside 100 ml of the reserved fish cooking liquid and add the rest of the liquid, peas, lemon juice and saffron to the pan. Simmer until reduced by half, about 10–15 minutes. Add half the butter and stir until melted. Season to taste. Pour into the baking dish and gently mix with the fish.

Once the potato and celeriac are soft, drain and let them cool for 2 minutes to allow some of the steam to evaporate. Add a little of the reserved fish cooking liquid until you can mash the vegetables to a smooth consistency. Season to taste.

Spread the mash over the top of the fish, roughing it up with a fork. This will give a crunchier end result. Melt the remaining butter and pour it evenly over the mash. Grate over some pecorino. Place the baking dish in the oven for 30 minutes or until the top is golden and crispy.

Remove from the oven and serve. Leftovers will keep for a few days in an airtight container in the fridge.

SPICE SHORTCUTS*

4½ tsp Gewürzhaus Fish Spice for Sauces

SWEET PAPRIKA
CORIANDER
FENNEL
YELLOW MUSTARD
ROSEMARY

Bavarian Roast Chicken

BAYERISCHES BRATHÄHNCHEN

Bavarian Roast Chicken Spice is, to this day, one of my all-time favourite Gewürzhaus spice blends. This recipe is based on that spice blend, recreating a similar version at home. The sweetness of the paprika matches so well with the chicken and lemon. When plated, it looks festive, and even better, it is simple and quick to prepare, which makes it perfect for hosting. – ***Eva***

SERVES 6
Gluten free / Dairy free

- 1 large chicken
- ½ tsp black peppercorns*
- ½ tsp yellow mustard seeds*
- ½ tsp coriander seeds*
- ¼ tsp fennel seeds*
- 100–120 ml extra-virgin olive oil
- 1½ tsp sweet paprika*
- ½ tsp salt flakes*
- 1 tsp finely chopped rosemary leaves*
- grated zest of 1 lemon
- lemon wedges, to serve

SPICE SHORTCUTS*
4¾ tsp Gewürzhaus Bavarian Roast Chicken Spice

Preheat the oven to 200°C fan-forced. Wash and dry the chicken inside and out.

Crush the peppercorns and mustard, coriander and fennel seeds well using a mortar and pestle. Transfer to a bowl. Add all the remaining ingredients, except the lemon wedges, and mix well.

Carefully separate the skin from the breast and the top of the drumsticks using your fingers, and rub the spice mixture in between the two. Next, rub the mixture over the surface of the chicken.

Place the chicken in a roasting tin, breast-side up, and add enough water to the bottom of the tin to cover the base before placing in the oven. Bake for 35–45 minutes, depending on the size of the chicken. While cooking, regularly spoon the pan juices over the chicken. Add more hot water to the dish if necessary.

Depending on your oven and your own personal taste, you may wish to increase the heat of the oven to 220°C fan-forced for the last 15 minutes to make the skin crispier.

Be sure to cook the chicken all the way through, but take it out of the oven while it is still moist. The best way to check if a roast chicken is cooked is by inserting a wooden skewer into the flesh – once the juices turn from reddish to clear, the chicken is ready.

Serve with lemon wedges and a classic side like the South German Potato Salad on page 126.

Peel off any leftover meat and store in an airtight container in the fridge for several days. You can use leftover chicken for sandwiches or to make a great risotto.

Oma's Nut Noodles

OMAS NUSSNUDELN

This dish is all about comfort and letting your inner child revel. Oma made this for us often and we loved it, smothering the noodles in the sugar and nut mixture. I still have her hand-crank nut mill that we freshly grind the walnuts with. These noodles are warming, crunchy, sweet, salty, nutty and delicious. Like having dessert for a main meal. – ***Eva***

SERVES 3–4
Vegetarian

- 250 g egg noodles (spaghetti or fettuccine are great)
- 100 g salted butter, roughly diced
- 2 tbsp extra-virgin olive oil
- 100 g (1⅔ cups) panko breadcrumbs
- ¾ tsp ground cassia, plus an extra ½ tsp to serve*
- ¼ tsp ground ginger*
- ¼ tsp ground allspice*
- ¼ tsp ground nutmeg*
- 80 g walnuts, coarsely ground
- 40 g white sugar

SPICE SHORTCUTS*
2 tsp Gewürzhaus Gingerbread Spice, Gewürzhaus St Nicholas Spekulaas Spice or Gewürzhaus Mixed Spice

Bring a large pot of salted water to the boil and cook the egg noodles as per the packet instructions, until al dente.

While the noodles are cooking, heat half the butter and half the oil in a large frying pan over medium heat for about 2 minutes, until the butter is melted and frothing. Add the breadcrumbs and spices and fry for about 5 minutes until golden brown, stirring regularly.

Drain the noodles and let them dry for a minute.

Add the noodles to the frying pan and toss them in the breadcrumb mixture. Add a little more butter and oil to the bottom of the pan by pushing the noodles aside, then spread them back out. Let them fry, without tossing, for approximately 2 minutes, until they form a crispy base. Gently turn them, add the remaining butter and oil and repeat this process. This will give you yummy crispy bits!

Mix the walnuts, sugar and extra cassia together in a small bowl.

Serve the noodles at the table and everyone can spoon over as much of the nut and sugar mixture as they like.

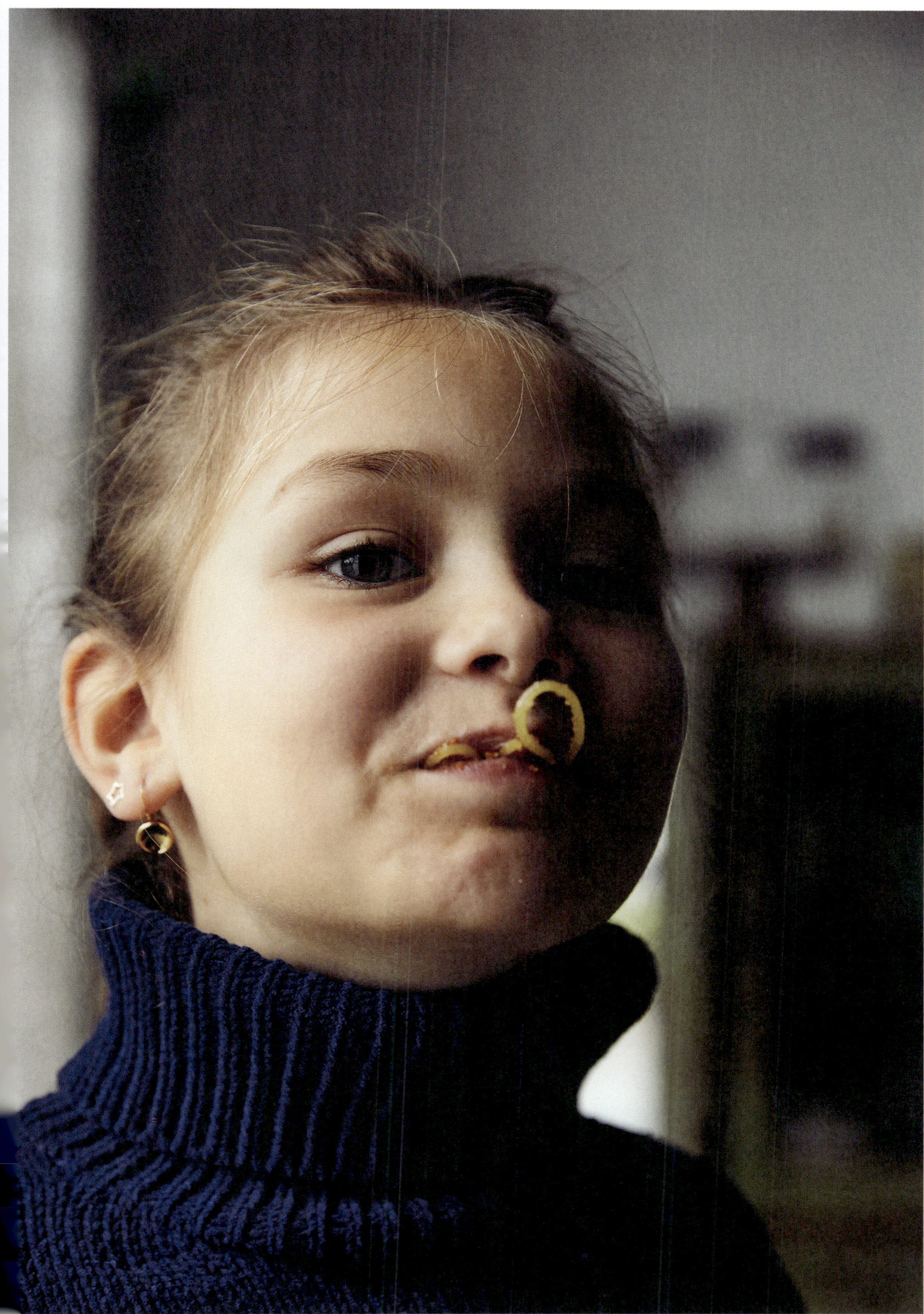

German Lentil & Ham Hock Soup

LINSENEINTOPF MIT EISBEIN

This is my spiced-up version of a German lentil soup, full of aromatics like allspice, juniper, star anise and bay, and warming on cold winter days. I make a big pot of it and freeze some for work lunches. – ***Maria***

SERVES 6
Gluten free

- 100 g salted butter
- 1 large onion, diced
- 1 leek, cut in half lengthways, finely sliced
- 1 carrot, diced
- 1 parsnip, diced
- 2 dried thyme sprigs (or 1 tsp dried thyme)
- 3 all-purpose potatoes, peeled and diced
- 1 x 1 kg ham or pork leg hock
- 5 allspice berries
- 2 star anise
- 2 juniper berries
- 1 fresh bay leaf
- 1 tsp fine Himalayan pink salt, plus extra
- ¼ tsp freshly cracked black pepper
- 290 g (1½ cups) brown lentils, soaked overnight in water with a pinch of salt
- 3 carrots, halved
- 1–2 tsp brown sugar
- 2–4 tsp apple cider vinegar
- leaves from 1 flat-leaf parsley sprig, roughly torn

Melt the butter in a large stockpot over medium–low heat and sauté the onion for about 8 minutes. Add the leek, carrot, parsnip and thyme and cook for a further 8 minutes. Finally, add the potato, ham hock, spices, bay leaf, salt, pepper and 3 litres of water. Bring the soup to a simmer and cook for 1 hour with the lid on.

Drain and rinse the lentils, then add them to the pot, along with the halved carrots, and cook for a further 45 minutes.

Fish out the spices, thyme stalks and bay leaf and discard in the compost. Transfer the ham to a large plate. Shred the meat by pressing down on it with a fork. (Set the fat and gristle aside to make *Schmalz*, page 80.) Discard the bone and return the meat to the soup.

Using a potato masher, mash some of the vegetables to thicken the soup to your liking. Season to taste with the brown sugar, apple cider vinegar, parsley and extra salt and pepper. Serve with crusty, buttered sourdough bread.

This soup will freeze well in portions. It will also keep in an airtight container in the fridge for up to 1 week.

Chicken Schnitzel with Lavender Crumb

HÜHNERSCHNITZEL MIT LAVENDELKRUSTE

Schnitzel was one of our most loved dinners as kids and is now constantly requested by our kids from their Oma Gabi. This version uses chicken breast instead of the more classic veal and is made more interesting and delicious by the addition of aniseed and lavender flower. Lavender, when uncooked, is potent, but it mellows and blends in really well in this schnitzel dish.

SERVES 4

- 2 large chicken breast fillets
- 2 pinches of aniseed*
- 3 pinches of coriander seeds*
- pinch of dried lavender flowers*
- 1¼ tsp sea salt flakes*
- 80 g (1 cup) breadcrumbs, made by blitzing stale sourdough bread in a food processor
- 75 g (½ cup) plain flour
- 1 egg, whisked together with a dash of full-cream milk
- extra-virgin olive oil, bacon fat or lard, for frying
- salted butter, for frying

SPICE SHORTCUTS*

1½ tsp Gewürzhaus French Lavender Salt

Cut each chicken fillet in half lengthways, horizontally. You should end up with four even-sized schnitzels. Pound these to a 5 mm thickness.

Using a mortar and pestle, grind the aniseed, coriander and lavender as finely as possible. Add the salt and breadcrumbs and gently mix together.

Line up three plates, and place the flour on the first, the whisked egg and milk on the second, and the breadcrumb mixture on the third.

Lightly but thoroughly coat each schnitzel in the flour on both sides. Shake off the excess. Dip each schnitzel in the egg, again coating both sides thoroughly, allowing the excess to drip off. Finally, dip each schnitzel in the breadcrumb mix, patting it on both sides to coat thoroughly.

Preheat a large heavy-based cast-iron frying pan over medium–low heat and add a generous amount of oil, fat or lard – enough to cover the base of the pan.

When the fat is hot, add a small knob of butter. Once it melts, fry the schnitzels until golden, approximately 2–3 minutes each side. Serve with a fresh, green salad, steamed, buttery potatoes and a wedge of lemon. Freeze uncooked schnitzels in an airtight container for 2 months.

Creamy Paprika Pork Traybake

SCHWEINESTEAKS IN PAPRIKA-RAHMSOßE

This dish is based on the forever-popular German meal of chicken in paprika-spiced cream. We grew up with this, and it is still served by family when we go back to Germany to visit. There are many companies that make a ready-mix for this that is sold widely in German supermarkets, but I wanted to come up with something as good in taste but without the additives. It is so easy to throw together mid-week and is ideal for making the most of the summer capsicum season. – ***Maria***

SERVES 4
Gluten free

- 500 ml (2 cups) thickened cream
- 2 tbsp tomato paste
- 600 g pork sirloin steaks, loin medallions or pork schnitzels, cut in half
- 1 red capsicum, deseeded and cut into strips
- 2 small red onions, halved and finely sliced

Herbs & spices

- 2 tbsp sweet paprika*
- ½ tsp smoked paprika*
- ¼ tsp freshly cracked black pepper*
- 1 tsp fine Himalayan pink salt*
- 1 tsp ground yellow mustard seeds*
- 1 tsp ground coriander seeds*
- ½ tsp ground fennel seeds*
- ½ tsp dried rosemary*
- 2 tsp dried summer savoury*

SPICE SHORTCUTS*
3½ tbsp Gewürzhaus Bavarian Roast Chicken Spice

Preheat the oven to 180°C fan-forced.

In a medium ovenproof dish, mix the cream and tomato paste with the herbs and spices until well combined. Add the pork, capsicum and onion and gently fold them into the cream mixture so they are fully coated. Press them down a little into the cream.

Bake in the oven for 35 minutes, checking towards the end of cooking that the top isn't burning. If it is, remove the dish briefly and push the meat and vegetables back down into the sauce.

Serve the traybake with buttered *Spätzle* (noodles), potatoes or spirelli pasta.

Leftovers will keep in an airtight container in the fridge for a few days.

COOK'S NOTES: *If you want to add more vegetables to this, I sometimes add two handfuls of cauliflower florets. It is also delicious with chicken thighs in place of the pork. If you don't have summer savoury, you could substitute with thyme.*

Cake

'On Sunday afternoons all over the country, ladies hosted a closed circle of carefully curated acquaintances for *Kaffee und Kuchen* (coffee and cake) in their homes. This ritual was recorded as far back as the 17th century and still occurs today, ingrained in the culture from north to south.'

Blue Poppy Crumble Cake

MOHNKUCHEN MIT STREUSELN

Poppy seeds are quintessential in German baking, used completely differently to the scant additions in Australian cakes. This cake has several steps, so make yourself a coffee and enjoy the process. – ***Eva***

SERVES 8
Vegetarian

- 200 g blue poppy seeds
- 100 ml full-cream milk
- 50 g salted butter
- 50 g white sugar

Base layer

- 170 g plain flour, plus extra
- 50 g white sugar
- 80 g salted butter, at room temp
- 1 egg
- ½ tsp baking powder

Filling

- 200 g sour cream
- 150 g cream cheese
- 150 g cottage cheese
- 100 g caster sugar
- 25 g cornflour
- seeds from 1 vanilla bean
- 1 tsp cardamom seeds, ground
- 1 tsp ground cassia
- 2 tbsp lemon juice
- 3 eggs

Crumble

- 70 g salted butter, cold
- 100 g plain flour
- 70 g white sugar
- ¼ tsp ground cassia

Process the poppy seeds in a poppy seed mill or food processor until they are crushed, but not ground.

In a small saucepan over medium heat, warm the milk, butter and sugar until almost at boiling point. Add the poppy seeds and cook for 2 minutes, stirring continuously. Remove from the heat, cover and set aside for 15 minutes.

To make the base layer, place all the ingredients in a mixing bowl and knead until a dough comes together. Turn out onto a bench and continue kneading until smooth, about 1 minute. Place in a ziplock bag and refrigerate for 30 minutes.

Preheat the oven to 160°C fan-forced. Line the base and side of a 23 cm round springform tin.

To make the filling, place all the ingredients, except the eggs, in a large mixing bowl with the poppy seed mixture. Beat until smooth using electric beaters. Add the eggs, one at a time, beating well after each addition. Set aside.

To make the crumble, dice the cold butter and place it in a bowl together with the remaining crumble ingredients. Using your fingertips, rub the mixture until it resembles panko breadcrumbs. Refrigerate.

Roll out the rested base dough on a lightly floured bench to a circle 23 cm in diameter. Transfer it to the cake tin and lightly press down. Use a fork to prick about 15 holes in the base. Add the filling and very lightly tap the tin on the bench so the filling settles. Bake in the oven for 40 minutes.

Remove the tin from the oven and add the crumble. Increase the oven temperature to 180°C fan-forced and bake the cake for a further 25 minutes. Remove from the oven and cool in the tin before turning out. Serve with a dollop of whipped cream.

Store leftovers in an airtight container in a cold spot for up to 1 week.

THE CULTURE OF KAFFEE UND KUCHEN

'It's a lovely way to connect and our hosts are always so proud to welcome us into their homes. The afternoons are slow and easy, the coffee and sugar keeping us in our seats for just that little bit longer.'

There's a word that us Germans are forever trying to translate: *gemütlich*. There really isn't anything like it in English that captures its essence in a single word. A Google search translates it to 'comfortable', 'cosy', 'homey', 'snug'. And that's some of the way there, but it's more than that. There is a depth required for something to be *gemütlich* – the environment needs to be just so – all of those words above but also quiet and peaceful, filled with love and care, beautiful in essence and easy to inhabit, inviting to meld into.

The Germans are, by and large, masters of *Gemütlichkeit*. Perhaps it's because of a combination of their love of detail, their overall tendency towards introversion and the climate they live in. Add to that their immense house pride, their exceeding frugality and their unrealistic expectations of hospitality establishments, and you have the ideal environment for the emergence and longevity of a national culture of *Kaffee und Kuchen* (coffee and cake).

On Sunday afternoons all over the country, ladies hosted a closed circle of carefully curated acquaintances for *Kaffee und Kuchen* in their homes. This ritual was recorded as far back as the 17th century and still occurs today, ingrained in the culture from north to south.

When our mother was a little girl, she remembers the excitement of visiting her cousins, Elke and Renate, in the big city of Hannover, where she and her family were invited for *Kaffee und Kuchen* every so often. Tante Liesel, her aunt, was a talented home seamstress, so Mum's cousins were always clothed in the latest fashionable '60s dresses, looking like they had stepped straight off the plane from London. Our mum was completely star struck. When they arrived in their Sunday best, there was always a *Frankfurter Kranz*, freshly baked by the lady of the house. It was Tante Liesel's signature cake, still talked about today and always made for *Kaffee und Kuchen*. They would sit around a beautifully set table, the adults drinking milky coffee out of fine china and everyone eating their piece of cake as politely and as straight-backed as possible.

Back at her childhood home, Mum tells of the commotion that engulfed the downstairs and upstairs residences when her parents and grandparents invited their friends on a Sunday. Couples would arrive in their best outfits, the children lined up to welcome the guests with a curtsy and bow. The ladies were then ushered upstairs to her grandparents' pristine apartment by her mum, Eva Viktoria, and her grandmother, Hannah, to take their seats at the table, which had been set with an embroidered tablecloth, homemade cakes, freshly whipped cream and the finest china they owned. Over cups of coffee, the ladies would chit-chat about all the goings-on of the town and their joint acquaintances. Our mum and her brother had to endure this until, finally, they were released and could dart down to the much more interesting and rambunctious sitting room, occupied by their father, Hans, their grandfather, Emil, and their guests.

There, you found beer and *Schnaps*, loosened ties and tobacco smoke so thick you could cut the air. The men's congregation bonded over endless games of *Skat* and lots of alcohol. This was their version of *Kaffee und Kuchen*. Mum's favourite guest was Uncle Otto with his fat cigars, who always sneaked the kids a much-coveted block of chocolate or even some money. As the men filled up with more and more *Schnaps*, the kids inched closer and closer, enchanted by the conversations their young ears were not really supposed to hear.

There are stories like these all over Germany, and they can be told by young and old. The endurance of the *Kaffee und Kuchen* culture is remarkable. It's morphed since those days to something less stiff and more homely. But, as all those years ago, if you are invited for a *Kaffee*, you never arrive to instant coffee at the kitchen bench. There will always be freshly brewed coffee and cake, perhaps bought from the local *Konditorei* if there is no time for baking. And you will always sit down at a table to share a story or catch up or become acquainted.

Whenever we go back to Germany to visit family and friends, we are greeted by invitation upon invitation for *Kaffee und Kuchen*. The afternoons are always *gemütlich*, the cake baked with love, the table set with thought, candles flickering and coffee brewing on the kitchen bench. It's a lovely way to connect, and our hosts are always so proud to welcome us into their homes. The afternoons are slow and easy, the coffee and sugar keeping us in our seats for just that little bit longer. Hours pass, many hours, and we feel like we were here only yesterday, partaking in this ritual with these same dear friends or family, when really, it's been years. We finally leave with a sense of ease and peace and wellbeing. We have connected and shared in another family's rhythm, and those memories we will hold and cherish until the next round of *Kaffee und Kuchen*.

BLUE POPPY CRUMBLE CAKE (PAGE 172), PISTACHIO & CHOCOLATE GINGERBREAD (PAGE 181)

GINGER
CASSIA
STAR ANISE
CORIANDER
NUTMEG

Pistachio & Chocolate Gingerbread

PISTAZIEN GEWÜRZKUCHEN MIT SCHOKOLADE

Luxurious yet light, this cake tastes like a European Christmas. It makes me want to curl up by the roaring fire, knitting project in hand, a tall glass of cold milk and a piece of this cake on the side table. Made with dates and honey, it's free from refined sugars and full of spices. I imagine this is much closer to the original gingerbreads that the Franconian monks made with their home-grown honey and cherished spices, bringing together therapeutic ingredients in a bread that would last a long time. – ***Maria***

SERVES 12–14
Gluten free / Vegetarian

- 140 g (¾ cup) dried pitted dates
- 180 g salted butter, at room temperature
- 250 g runny honey
- 3 eggs
- 100 g (1 cup) ground almonds
- 150 g buckwheat flour
- 1½ tsp bicarbonate of soda
- 3 tsp ground cassia*
- 3 tsp ground coriander seeds*
- 2½ tsp ground star anise*
- 1 tbsp ground ginger*
- 1 tsp ground nutmeg*
- ½ tsp vanilla extract
- finely grated zest of 1 orange
- finely grated zest of 1 lemon
- 90 g dark chocolate (85% cocoa), grated
- 250 ml (1 cup) full-cream milk
- 65 g raw shelled pistachios

SPICE SHORTCUTS*
3 tbsp + 1½ tsp Gewürzhaus Gingerbread Spice, plus 1 tsp ground ginger

Preheat the oven to 160°C fan-forced. Line the base and side of a 25 cm round springform tin.

Process the dates in a food processor for only a few seconds on high speed, until they are broken down into very small pieces, but not yet turning into a paste. Set aside.

Using electric beaters, cream the butter and honey in a large bowl, about 1½ minutes. Be careful to not over-cream as the mixture can split. Add the eggs, one at a time, beating well after each addition. Add the dates and beat in briefly.

In a separate bowl, combine the almonds, flour, bicarbonate of soda, spices, vanilla, zests and chocolate. Add a few heaped tablespoons of the dry mix to the butter mix and fold it in. Add a dash of milk to the butter mix and fold in. Continue, alternating between the two, finishing with dry mix. Transfer the batter to the tin and smooth out the top.

Place the pistachios on a clean tea towel, then fold the tea towel over to cover them. Using the base of a jar or something similar, crush the pistachios until you have a mixture of small and large pieces, but not too small. Sprinkle the pistachios over the top of the cake batter.

Bake for 25–30 minutes, until a skewer inserted into the centre of the cake comes out clean. Cool in the tin before turning out onto a serving plate. Store in an airtight container in a cool spot for up to 10 days.

COOK'S NOTES: *You can turn this into a birthday cake by pouring over a layer of chocolate ganache. To make the ganache, heat 200 ml of thickened cream and pour it over 100 g of dark chocolate, broken into small pieces in a bowl. Stir until the chocolate is melted, then pour over the cooled cake. Instead of topping the cake batter with pistachios before baking, sprinkle some chopped roasted pistachios over the ganache.*

Classic German Apple Cake

KLASSISCHER APFELKUCHEN

As a child, our mother spent her summers in their huge garden with an old apple orchard. In autumn, when the apples were harvested, everyone had to help, and they were made into apple sauce or apple juice. Money was tight in the late 1950s and early 1960s and nothing went to waste. The children participated unwillingly, much preferring to use the apples to throw at each other when playing in the orchard with neighbourhood friends, making sure their parents would not witness this wasteful behaviour. Our grandmother, Eva, whom I am named after, also made a version of this apple cake. Unfortunately, we don't have her original recipe, but Mum says this is pretty close. – ***Eva***

SERVES 10
Vegetarian

- 150 g salted butter, at room temperature, plus 30 g melted butter
- 150 g white sugar
- 3 eggs
- 3 tsp ground cassia*
- ¼ tsp ground cloves*
- ¼ tsp ground nutmeg*
- 1 tsp dried rose petals, crushed by rubbing between your fingertips*
- 150 g (1 cup) self-raising flour
- 75 g (¾ cup) ground almonds
- 1–2 tbsp full-cream milk, if needed
- 4–5 small to medium apples
- 2–3 tsp icing sugar
- ice cream, cream or custard, to serve

SPICE SHORTCUTS*
4½ tsp Gewürzhaus Apple Cake Spice

Preheat the oven to 180°C fan-forced. Grease and flour a 23 cm round springform cake tin and tap out the excess flour.

Using electric beaters, cream the butter and sugar in a large bowl for about 5 minutes, then add the eggs, one at a time, beating well after each addition. Once combined, add the spices and rose petals and beat thoroughly for a few minutes.

Sift in the flour and add the ground almonds, then beat until combined. The batter should be quite firm. However, if it is too stiff, you may need to add a few tablespoons of milk to loosen it. Spread the batter evenly into the prepared tin.

Peel the apples, cut them in half and remove the cores. With their flat-sides down, cut slits a few millimetres apart into each apple half, stopping just shy of the centre. Take care not to cut right through.

Place the apple halves, slit-side up, in a circle around the edge of the cake, with one in the middle, and gently press them 5 mm into the batter. Brush the apple with some of the melted butter and bake for about 30 minutes.

Remove the cake from the oven and brush with the remaining melted butter, then bake for a further 10–15 minutes, until golden brown. Insert a wooden skewer into the centre of the cake and if it comes out clean, the cake is cooked.

Cool in the tin for 15 minutes, then transfer to a wire rack. When the cake is cold, shake the icing sugar over it with a sieve.

The cake is best served with ice cream, cream or custard. It will keep for 1 week in an airtight container stored in a cool place.

COOK'S NOTES: *To make this gluten free, replace the flour with buckwheat flour and add 2–3 tsp gluten-free baking powder.*

Spiked Brown Cherry Cake

BESCHWIPSTER BRAUNER KIRSCHKUCHEN

Cherries have a strong place on our food line. Our mum had a sour cherry and a sweet cherry tree in her garden as a child, big old trees before the days of dwarf grafting. They collected cherries in a reed basket every year, our grandfather and great-grandfather up a wooden ladder, the three kids responsible for collecting what they could reach from the ground. When you bit into a cherry, they *knacked*, they were so fresh. Our mum still remembers that moment. This cake is an ode to that childhood. Of cherries and chocolate and sweet sticky syrup, and parents on the verandah with a glass of *Kirschwasser* and a deck of cards. – ***Maria***

SERVES 10
Vegetarian

- 140 g salted butter, at room temperature
- 50 g coconut sugar
- 4 eggs, separated
- 3 tbsp maple syrup
- 2 tsp ground cinnamon
- ½ tsp ground allspice
- pinch of freshly cracked black pepper
- 90 g dark chocolate (85% cocoa), grated
- 150 g (1½ cups) ground almonds
- 50 g (½ cup) dried breadcrumbs
- 1 × 680 g jar pitted morello cherries, drained, liquid reserved
- double cream, to serve

Spiked syrup

- reserved cherry juice (see above)
- 2 tbsp raw sugar
- 1 cinnamon quill
- 8 black peppercorns
- pinch of salt
- Kirschwasser

Preheat the oven to 170°C conventional. Grease and flour a 23 cm round springform tin and tap out the excess flour.

Using electric beaters, cream the butter and sugar. Add one egg yolk at a time, beating well after each addition. Beat in the maple syrup and spices, then fold in the chocolate.

In a separate bowl, beat the egg whites until stiff. Fold half the egg whites into the butter mixture, followed by half the ground almonds and half the breadcrumbs. Repeat with the other half.

Transfer the batter to the prepared tin and smooth over. Place the cherries evenly across the top, then gently press them into the batter with a spatula. Run the spatula around the cake on an angle to smooth some batter over the tops of the cherries – they should be just submerged and semi-covered.

Bake for 25–30 minutes, until a skewer comes out clean. Let the cake completely cool before turning out. Ideally, let it rest for 3–4 hours or overnight, in an airtight container.

To make the syrup, place the reserved cherry juice and sugar in a saucepan over low heat, stirring to dissolve the sugar. Once dissolved, add the spices and salt and increase the heat to bring the mixture to the boil. Reduce the heat to a fast simmer and cook for 15–25 minutes, until lightly thickened. Remove from the heat and cool for 15 minutes. Stir through a generous swig of *Kirschwasser*. The mixture will continue to thicken as it cools, so don't let it thicken too much on the stove.

Serve with double cream and a drizzle of spiked syrup on top.

COOK'S NOTES: *This cake is best made the night before. The flavours meld and the cherries give off their lovely juices when the cake is left to cure for a while. If you don't have coconut sugar, you can use brown sugar.* Kirschwasser *is a clear, high-alcohol spirit that is often drunk as an apéritif.*

BAKING A BIRTHDAY CAKE

'Baking cakes and throwing a party for my girls is a labour of love, of appreciation. It's my way of saying "You're special and deserve to be celebrated". It's important to me to give my time for that.'

To us, birthdays have always felt special. Our mum brought both family and friends together for our birthdays, and we always felt celebrated. We are both December babies – our birthdays fall within days of Christmas – and I wonder whether Mum made even more of a point of celebrating them, so that our important days wouldn't be lost in the busyness of the festive season.

I'm not too sure whether Mum had birthday cakes as a child or if the tradition really started with the *Women's Weekly Children's Birthday Cakes* book, but every year we got to choose a princess with rosettes, a train with popcorn or some other wonderful creation from that magical book, which Mum would then spend hours baking and decorating, often with the help of her mother-in-law, our grandmother, Oma Liesel.

In the years before we moved to Australia and pre the *Birthday Cake* book era, Mum would bake a traditional German cake called *Marmorkuchen*. It's a simple yet stunning creation. This cake uses a one-bowl dough that is uncomplicated and reasonably foolproof to make. Half of the dough is flavoured with chocolate, then the two are swirled together and baked in a *Gugelhupf* cake tin, which highlights the beautiful patterns of the entangled colours. The marbling of the vanilla and chocolate doughs, when cut, are a favourite with all kids, and a rich ganache topping complements the moistness of the cake. Decorating this cake is also simple: either with candles, some bunting or even a few toy animals to create a zoo theme. It works for both young and old.

Celebrating birthdays with two daughters who are growing up in a more tech-savvy world means they spend weeks, sometimes months, in the lead-up to their birthday, scanning Pinterest for the perfect cake. My reaction sits somewhere between terror and excitement when they show me what I am to create.

These days we celebrate birthdays in a pretty big way in my family – with three cakes! Yes, three! The cake for school – because having your class sit around your creation, candles alight and singing Happy Birthday in both German and English, feels pretty special. Then, there is the kids' party, complete with a jumping castle, sleepover or whatever my kids can convince me of being fun yet reasonable. Here, their Pinterest dreams come true: I go all out with the cake and have made everything, from a fairy castle to Ariel in a shell with Sebastian and Flounder – all carefully pieced together from fondant – to the Hungry Caterpillar or a unicorn with marshmallows. I treat this like more of a craft project than baking, and the end result is always a surprise. When the kids see their cake they cannot contain their excitement, each picking different elements they want to devour. The parents at the party look at me in disbelief; yes, at times I can be quite an overachiever, but I enjoy this process and am proud of what I create for them. Lastly, there is the family birthday with cousins, aunties, uncles and grandparents, which is a calmer get-together, often on the actual birthday, with thoughtful presents and a slow pace.

This is where I now bake the *Marmorkuchen*, a reminder of my childhood and something beautiful that does not need to be time-consuming or complicated.

Baking cakes and throwing a party for my girls is a labour of love, of appreciation. It's my way of saying 'You're special and deserve to be celebrated'. It's important to me to give my time for that. Their dad celebrates them in his own way; every year, for their birthdays, he takes them on a date night. It's a special time for just them to have together. I know they value this ritual because every year, they go back to their favourite restaurant, wanting to repeat the specialness of the previous year. They don't choose somewhere new – they choose the place where they have put down birthday roots, together with their dad.

When I celebrate my birthday with family and friends, I feel very loved and appreciated. The kind words written on cards, the thoughtful gifts, the long and tight 'hello' cuddles. It is a time for laughter and fun, a meal shared, a cake baked, candles blown out and a wish made, a little dance and a coming together of all those most important to me, to celebrate me and the life I'm living. Throughout the year, we give much to others, willingly with love and care, but, on this day, it feels good to receive.

The reason I create rituals or carry on those from my childhood is that I want the girls to be anchored to them when they grow up, to be connected back to their family. It doesn't matter to me whether the rituals have been handed down through generations or I create them myself. The important thing is that they are the times in the year when we all gather. And, in the years to come, when my girls have left home, they will know that we all get back together. That they belong.

– Eva

Chocolate Marble Cake

MARMORKUCHEN

Other than creating elaborate birthday cakes, when it comes to cooking and baking, I really love no-fuss home cooking: nothing too finicky or time consuming, not too much washing up and, ideally, a realistic ingredients list. This cake is the perfect balance between looking special, being easy to bake and tasting moist, chocolatey and delicious. You can even cut out one step and instead of making the glaze, just dust it with icing sugar. – ***Eva***

SERVES 10
Vegetarian

300 g (2 cups) plain flour, plus extra for dusting

3 tsp baking powder

300 g salted butter, softened

250 g white sugar

5 eggs

200 g plain yoghurt

1–2 tbsp full-cream milk, if needed

80 g dark chocolate (60–70% cocoa), broken into pieces

1 tbsp ground cassia*

½ tsp ground ginger*

½ tsp ground allspice*

½ tsp ground nutmeg*

½ tsp ground cloves*

Glaze

150 g dark chocolate (60–70% cocoa), broken into pieces

80 ml thickened cream

SPICE SHORTCUTS*
1½ tbsp Gewürzhaus Mixed Spice

Preheat the oven to 160°C fan-forced. Grease and flour a 23 cm *Gugelhupf* (bundt) cake tin and tap out the excess flour.

Sift the flour and baking powder into a bowl.

Using electric beaters on medium–high, cream the butter and sugar in a large bowl for 5 minutes or until pale and fluffy. Add the eggs, one by one, beating in between each addition.

Add 3 heaped tablespoons of the flour mixture to the creamed butter and sugar and beat until fully incorporated. Add 3 heaped tablespoons of the yoghurt to the mixture and beat it in well. Repeat until both the flour mixture and yoghurt are used up and fully incorporated into the batter. If it is too stiff, add a few tablespoons of milk to loosen it. Add half the batter to the cake tin and set aside.

Melt the chocolate in the microwave on high in 30-second bursts, stirring in between, until fully melted. Gently fold the melted chocolate and spices into the remaining batter. Add the chocolate batter to the cake tin then, using a fork, mix the two doughs together in a circular motion to slightly combine them and give it a marbled effect.

Bake in the oven for about 40 minutes or until a skewer inserted in the centre of the cake comes out clean. Allow the cake to cool in the tin for 10 minutes, then turn it out onto a wire rack and leave it to cool.

To make the glaze, warm the chocolate and cream in a small saucepan over low heat, whisking continuously until melted and glossy. Pour the hot mixture over the cooled cake.

Store in an airtight container in a cool spot for up to 1 week.

PICTURED ON PAGE 186

Sigrid's Rhubarb Cake with Coconut Meringue Hood

SIGRIDS RHABARBERKUCHEN MIT KOKOSHAUBE

One of my earliest memories of rhubarb is of watching a friend of my mum's peeling long stalks of freshly picked rhurbarb in her sunny kitchen. I was mesmerised. What was that beautiful, gleaming thing she was peeling? I've since had a great love for rhubarb, and have grown it in every garden I've inhabited, as is done in Germany. It's one of my favourite fruits to bake into sweet dishes.

This recipe is inspired by my godmother Sigrid's famous rhubarb cake. She is an excellent baker and a real master of *Kaffee und Kuchen*, setting her table with love and detail and, of course, delicious homemade cake. Every time we visit her on a trip to Germany, we hope she will make her version of this cake. – ***Maria***

SERVES 10
Vegetarian

Spiced rhubarb

- 800 g peeled rhubarb stems, chopped into 2 cm pieces
- 1 tsp ground cassia*
- ½ tsp ground allspice*
- ½ tsp ground ginger*
- pinch each of sea salt flakes and freshly cracked black pepper
- 1 tbsp raw sugar

Base

- 100 g salted butter, at room temperature
- 70 g (⅓ cup) raw sugar
- 1 tsp vanilla extract, or seeds scraped from ½ vanilla bean
- 1 egg, plus 2 egg yolks
- 150 g (1 cup) plain flour
- 50 g (½ cup) tapioca starch
- 2 tsp baking powder
- 1 tbsp full-cream milk

To prepare the spiced rhubarb, place all the ingredients in a medium saucepan with 125 ml (½ cup) of water and mix to combine. Cover with a lid and cook over medium–low heat for 12 minutes, stirring regularly. Drain the liquid into a bowl and set aside to make a refreshing rhubarb drink (page 192).

Preheat the oven to 180°C conventional and line a 23 cm round springform tin.

To make the base, using electric beaters, cream the butter and sugar in a large bowl for about 5 minutes. Add the vanilla, egg and egg yolks, one at a time, beating well after each addition, but being careful that the mixture does not split. Add the dry ingredients and fold them into the batter. Finally, add the milk and fold it in.

Transfer the batter to the prepared tin. Fill a mug three-quarters full with boiling water. Heat a tablespoon in the water. Using the back of the hot spoon, spread the batter evenly in the tin, returning the spoon to the hot water periodically to reheat it.

Spread the rhubarb evenly over the batter, pressing down a little. Bake in the oven for 20 minutes.

About 15 minutes into the baking time, prepare the coconut meringue layer. Beat the egg whites until stiff. While continuing to beat, add a tablespoon of sugar at a time. Add the coconut and fold it gently into the egg white.

CONTINUED OVERLEAF >

Coconut meringue

2 egg whites

3 tbsp raw sugar

75 g (1¼ cups) shredded coconut

To serve

double cream

SPICE SHORTCUTS*

2 tsp Gewürzhaus Mixed Spice

COOK'S NOTES: *If you don't have tapioca starch, you can use cornflour instead.*

Remove the cake from the oven after 20 minutes of baking and add the meringue layer by carefully but quickly spooning on dollops of the mixture. Gently even it out, then return the cake to the oven. Bake for a further 15 minutes or until the meringue is golden brown and a skewer inserted comes out clean.

Allow the cake to cool completely in the tin before turning out. This cake is best served the next day, as the rhubarb has time to develop its flavour. Serve with a dollop of double cream.

Store in an airtight container in a cool place for up to 1 week.

—

Refreshing Rhubarb Shrub

You can use the drained liquid from the spiced rhubarb to make a shrub. This shrub is so easy to make and is the most refreshing mixer to drink in summer.

Transfer the cooled liquid into a clear, sterilised jar or bottle (see page 29 for instructions) and mark the level on the side with a marker. Add an equal amount of apple cider vinegar (with the mother). Mark again. Finally, add another equal amount of honey. Close the lid and shake the jar vigorously until the honey is dissolved, about 2 minutes. Once dissolved, store in the fridge for several months.

To serve, pour a dash of shrub into a glass and top with sparkling water. It's also great in a cocktail or with gin or vodka in a mixer.

A CAKE THAT RUNS IN THE FAMILY

'One torte stood out from the many in Rosa's repertoire: the *Dobosch*. Twelve individually baked layers of thin sponge stacked on top of each other with a filling of chocolate buttercream between each layer.'

Our paternal great-grandmother, Rosalia, was a wedding cake baker in the tiny village of Sanktanna, Romania, where her German ancestors settled as Banat Swabians in the 18th century. Our cousin once removed tells the story of what it was like to live in Romania in the late 1960s after the war was over, before electricity came to their village. There was relative peace; the men and women who were sent to war and reconstruction camps having returned. There was time for lying in the meadows in the afternoon sun, finally time for love to flourish again, and so there were weddings to celebrate.

A Sanktanna wedding was an elaborate and generous affair when it came to food and drink. A usual wedding went something like this: before the wedding party and villagers' ritualistic walk to the church, guests were served salted crescents, biscuits and *Schnaps*. After the church service, half a dozen different cakes, more *Schnaps*. A light lunch of broth with noodles or rice and chicken in tomato sauce. Afternoon tea was warm cheesecake out of the oven. Dinner was served at about 6 pm – chicken, veal and pork with half a dozen accompaniments. Sweets at 7 pm – ten different tortes and about 30 (!) different slices, cakes and biscuits. At 1 am, guests were treated to filled cabbage or sausages with mustard, plus a roast with cabbage salad and preserved fruit. Finally, in the wee hours of the morning, each wedding guest, giddy from dancing and *Schnaps*, was sent home with a wide selection of the leftover sweets.

Oma Rosa's part in this was the ten tortes. These were elaborate, multi-layered creations of cream and caramel and icing. They were among the highlights of the celebratory feast, standing tall amid the sea of slices, biscuits and cakes. They were what was talked about afterwards. 'The *Nylontorte* was excellent.' 'Hmm, yes, just the right amount of coffee in it.' All would nod in unison if the baker had done their job well.

With no electric beaters, let alone a stand mixer, the job of making these ten tortes was no small or fast feat. About 90 eggs needed beating by hand. Rosa had some help – our Oma Liesel and her two sisters, as well as their adolescent daughters, were all put to work with whisks or forks and bowls filled with egg whites. Our dad, the only male in the congregation of women, had the easy job of carrying the finished cakes down to the cellar, where they awaited their transport to the house of the wedding party. The younger women of the family tell stories of hard work and aching arms. Days of beating and whisking and baking.

One torte stood out from the many in Rosa's repertoire: the *Dobosch*. Twelve individually baked layers of thin sponge, stacked on top of each other, with a filling of chocolate buttercream between each layer. The outside was clad in more buttercream, then decorated with either a hard burnt-toffee disc that was marked with cut lines for a hot knife to be used on later, or piped rosettes of more buttercream. The sugar syrup was tested with a looped piece of wire, which was dipped into the syrup – if a bubble could be blown, the syrup was done.

This practice never changed, even with the arrival of candy thermometers, and we were fascinated by this process as kids. This torte stood out for good reason: it was unlike anything else Oma Rosa made, impressive in stature and embedded work. It was really quite a job to create it.

Not only was it made for weddings, Rosa and her daughters made a *Dobosch* for every significant birthday or celebration in the family. We both recall, like it was yesterday, the discussions that would precede the baking of a *Dobosch* in our grandmother's tiny apartment in northern Germany many years later, where Rosa – then close to 100 years old – and her three daughters debated the merits of the different flavours of buttercream, a decision needing to be made as to which was most suitable for the occasion. A significant birthday celebration was not complete without a *Dobosch*. In fact, in the circle of people from the days of our youth, there would have been a palpable discomfort should the *Dobosch* have been missing.

We are now the fourth generation making *Dobosch* to mark important events in our lives. Both of our weddings in Australia were graced with a *Dobosch*, the centrepiece of the *Kaffee und Kuchen* ritual (page 175) we both incorporated into the celebrations, and every few years, one is made for a significant birthday. Soon, our children will learn.

It's important for us to carry on the making of this cake, because in the motions of its making lie memories, happy ones. As we carefully spread the sponge batter onto a baking tray, we hear Oma Rosa in our ear: 'Not too thick! Not too thin!' And we smile and feel peaceful. We know where we come from. We are reminded, as bittersweet as it is, that we are here for only a period of time, that we will come and go, like Oma Rosa, and that we are blessed to have been equipped to celebrate and mark the passing of time in such a meaningful and connected way.

Our Great-Grandmother's 12-Layered Chocolate Buttercream Cake

OMA ROSAS SCHOKOLADEN DOBOSCHTORTE

Our great-grandmother, Rosalia Becker, was a wedding cake baker and made tortes for the receptions in the village. Weddings had an assortment of cakes and on average 90 eggs were used to bake for just one festivity. Our father recalls having to endlessly carry cakes down into the earthen cellar and back out for the celebrations. This cake was my favourite as a child and is 'the' cake in our family line. – ***Eva***

SERVES 12
Vegetarian

12 eggs

12 tbsp white sugar

1 vanilla bean, split and seeds scraped out

12 tbsp plain flour, plus extra for dusting

¼ tsp baking powder

Chocolate buttercream

200 g dark chocolate (60–70% cocoa)

300 g white sugar

3 eggs

350 g butter, at room temperature

Heat the oven to 180°C fan-forced. Prepare two round baking trays by buttering and dusting them with flour. I use the bases of springform cake tins for this – they must be at least 26 cm in diameter. Alternatively, trace two 26 cm circles on baking paper and line regular baking trays.

Separate six eggs, placing the whites in a large mixing bowl and the yolks in a smaller one. Using electric beaters, whisk the egg whites until quite stiff, then add 5 tablespoons of the sugar, one at a time, beating well after each addition, until fully incorporated.

Add 1 tablespoon of the sugar and the seeds from the vanilla bean to the egg yolks and whisk with electric beaters until fluffy, about 1 minute. Add the egg yolk mixture to the egg white mixture and very gently fold in until just combined. Sieve 6 tablespoons of the flour and half the baking powder over the egg mixture and, using a whisk, gently fold in until just incorporated. The goal is to keep the mixture as fluffy as possible.

Next, take one-sixth of this mixture and carefully spread it evenly onto the prepared baking tray, forming a 26 cm diameter circle. The circle should be approximately 5 mm thick. Repeat with another one-sixth of the mixture and the second baking tray.

Place in the oven and cook for 8 minutes or until golden. Remove from the oven and, with care, immediately remove the cake layers from the trays and place them on wire racks. Again, prepare the trays with butter and flour – you may need to wipe them down before doing so – and repeat until you have six layers of cake rounds.

CONTINUED OVERLEAF >

Repeat making the batter with the remaining ingredients and cooking six more discs so you have 12 layers of cake. (If you make the batter all at once, it deflates too much and the layers won't be right.)

Next, make the chocolate buttercream. Break the chocolate into pieces and place in a heatproof bowl. Microwave on high in 30-second bursts, stirring in between, until melted and smooth. Set aside.

Place the sugar and 3 tablespoons of water in a small saucepan and set aside. Separate the eggs, placing the whites in one mixing bowl and the yolks in another. Place the pan with the sugar and water over high heat and immediately start whisking the egg whites in the bowl, using electric beaters, until stiff.

Now turn your attention back to the sugar syrup, which will be starting to become clear. Using a candy thermometer, heat it to 120°C, without stirring. As soon as it reaches this temperature, take the pan off the heat and start slowly pouring the syrup into the egg whites, a little at a time, beating on medium speed after each addition, until well combined. Try not to pour the syrup directly onto the beater, but down the side of the bowl as the sugar syrup is very hot. Repeat until the syrup is fully incorporated.

Add the melted chocolate, then turn the mixer to high and continue to beat until the mixture has cooled down, about 5–10 minutes.

Next, add the butter to the bowl with the egg yolks and beat until fluffy.

Transfer a heaped teaspoon of the egg yolk and butter mixture to the bowl of egg whites and, on medium speed, mix until fully incorporated. Keep adding the butter mixture, a spoonful at a time, until you have used it all up.

Finally, we get to the assembling of the cake. Divide the buttercream into thirds – one-third is for the top and side and the other two-thirds are for the layers.

Place one layer of the cake on a cake stand and spread some of the buttercream over it (about an eleventh of the mixture you set aside for the layers). It can be a little hard to judge how much to use here. It should cover the cake layer just enough so that you can't see the cake underneath. Place the next layer of cake on top and gently press it down. Spread more buttercream over it and repeat until all the layers are complete, except the top layer, which you leave uncovered.

Before spreading buttercream on the top layer, trim the edge of the cake, the whole way around, into a nice and smooth round shape – kind of like cutting the crusts off toast! Lastly, spread buttercream over the top and side of the cake and smooth it out as much as possible. Any remaining mixture can be piped onto the top as decoration.

Refrigerate the cake for 24 hours and make sure you bring it back to room temperature before serving.

COOK'S NOTES: *You need to work gently yet quickly with the cake batter, so it stays fluffy and does not deflate. Ideally it is made a day in advance so the buttercream can soften the layers. If you prefer coffee flavouring, you can substitute the chocolate for a shot of strong espresso to make a coffee buttercream instead.*

Spaghetti Ice Cream

SPAGHETTI EIS

Germany has a culture of eating ice cream. Lots of it. In places known as *Eisdielen*. Whatever you order, expect it to be monstrous in size and completely kitsch. Expect multiple scoops, mounds of whipped cream, sickly sweet toppings and a cocktail umbrella for good measure. *Spaghetti Eis* is one of the options found on menus in these ice cream cafés. Our family friend, Arnold, would take me and Eva to have this special treat when we visited from Australia, regardless of the freezing temperatures outside. Mum was not allowed to pack us in the car until this ritual had been observed and oh, we loved this so much. *Spaghetti Eis* is usually served as an individual portion, but this recipe makes an impressively large bowl of it. My son orders it for his birthday dessert and is always giddy with excitement at the magic of eating sweet 'noodles' with strawberry sauce and faux parmesan. – ***Maria***

SERVES 6–8
Gluten free / Vegetarian

1 litre soft, airy vanilla ice cream

grated white chocolate, to serve

Strawberry sauce

250 g strawberries, hulled and quartered

1½ tbsp vanilla sugar

¾ tsp balsamic vinegar

pinch of sea salt flakes

Vanilla cream

200 ml thickened cream

2 tsp vanilla sugar

Place a potato ricer with a coarse disc in the freezer or fridge.

To make the strawberry sauce, gently cook the strawberries in a small saucepan over low heat for 8–10 minutes, stirring regularly. When they are soft and mushy, transfer to a food processor. Add the sugar, vinegar and salt, then blitz until you have a smooth sauce. Place in the fridge to cool completely.

For the vanilla cream, place the cream in a large bowl and, using electric beaters, whisk until stiff peaks form. Beat in the sugar. Gently dollop the cream in the middle of a large serving plate, then smooth it over with a spatula so you have a flat-topped mound. Place in the freezer for an hour or so to give the cream a nice cold edge to crack through and to help the ice cream to not melt too fast.

To assemble, fill the potato ricer barrel with ice cream. Press the ice cream out through the ricer onto the mound of cream, starting at the edge of the cream. Twist the plate a little as you press to give the look of twirled spaghetti. Repeat until you have completely covered the cream in ice cream spaghetti. Pour the cold strawberry sauce over the spaghetti. Finish with a grating of white chocolate.

Serve immediately before the ice cream melts. Store leftovers in an airtight container in the freezer for a few weeks.

COOK'S NOTES: *Fluffy and fresh ice cream will go through the potato ricer more easily than dense ice cream, so buy it fresh just before you need it and experiment with different brands. You might also need to take the ice cream out of the freezer and put it in the fridge before you press it, so it is soft enough to go through.*

Easter

'After the egg hunt, we start preparing the food. First, we roll out the yeast dough I prepared in the morning, smear on the chocolate filling and then braid the delicious Easter bread. We eat it warm out of the oven, ripping off large chunks … For lunch we set the table with thought and care and sit together as a family to share a meal. Mum usually joins us, too. It is often slow-roasted lamb with roast vegetables and delicious sauces. Nothing fancy, nor overly formal, just a meal that is conducive to spending time together.'

Warm Chocolate Easter Braid

SCHOKOLADEN HEFEZOPF

This is most definitely best eaten straight out of the oven – the warmth of the bread and gooeyness of the chocolate is just irresistible. If you're well versed in making yeast dough, this recipe will be easy to follow and the braiding quite fun to create. You'll be sure to impress everyone at the table. If you'd like to be experimental, play around with different fillings such as nuts or poppy seeds. We make this bread every Easter Sunday as a breakfast treat to add to the already crazy chocolate hit awaiting us on this day. – ***Eva***

SERVES 6–8
Vegetarian

300 g (2 cups) 00 flour, plus extra for dusting

25 g fresh yeast

170 ml full-cream milk, lukewarm

30 g white sugar

pinch of fine Himalayan pink salt

2 tbsp extra-virgin olive oil, plus extra for coating the dough

2 egg yolks

Chocolate filling

125 g salted butter

100 g white sugar

1 vanilla bean, split and seeds scraped out

2 heaped tbsp cocoa*

½ tsp ground cardamom*

Glaze

1 egg, lightly beaten

SPICE SHORTCUTS*

2 tbsp + ½ tsp Gewürzhaus Chocolate Spice

Place the flour in a mixing bowl and create a well in the centre. Crumble the yeast into the well and add half the milk, the sugar and salt. Gently mix, incorporating a little of the flour as you go. Sprinkle a thin layer of flour over the milk, cover the bowl with a damp tea towel and place in a warm spot for 20 minutes. After this time, the yeast should be bubbling. Add the oil, egg yolks and remaining milk and mix with a fork, working from the inside out, slowly incorporating all the flour. When it's too difficult to mix with the fork, use your hands to scoop up the dough from the outside and fold it into the centre. Once it starts coming together, turn it out onto a lightly floured bench and knead into a soft dough, about 5 minutes.

Flour a clean bowl, lightly rub the dough with oil, then place it into the bowl. Dust with flour again and cover with a damp tea towel. Place in a warm spot for 1 hour or until the dough has doubled in size.

To make the filling, place all the ingredients in a small saucepan and melt over low heat for 2 minutes, stirring well. Cool slightly in the fridge – the mixture should still be spreadable.

When the dough is ready, turn it out onto a lightly floured bench and briefly knead, then cut into three equal parts. Roll out each piece into a rectangle, about 30–40 cm long and 15–20 cm wide. Spread one-third of the filling over each rectangle. Tightly roll up each rectangle from the long side.

Once you have three long rolls, gently pinch them together at one end, then braid them together. Tuck the ends in a little, then carefully transfer to a greased and flour-dusted loaf tin. Rest for a further 20 minutes.

In the meantime, preheat the oven to 180°C fan-forced.

Brush the braid with the beaten egg to glaze it, then bake for 25 minutes. Let the braid rest in the tin to cool slightly. Turn it out and serve it by pulling off large pieces. Best eaten fresh.

Super Twix Bars

SUPER TWIX RIEGEL

Chocolate has steadily worked its way into the Easter traditions of much of the world. Despite it having nothing to do with Easter per se, it's here to stay and brings with it much joy and anticipation. The milk chocolate of most Easter eggs is overly sweet for my palate, yet a bar of the usual dark chocolate doesn't cut it when you have those sugar-laden offerings around. This recipe came about as I wanted to make something moreish and nutritious, that I would reach for over and above those eggs. These bars, similar to a Twix, now have a permanent place in our fridge. They are packed full of sustaining fats and have a satisfying sweetness from the dates. You will have trouble believing that they are not full of processed sugars. – ***Maria***

MAKES 40
Gluten free / Vegetarian

Base

150 g (1½ cups) ground almonds
50 g brown rice flour
1½ tsp ground cinnamon
80 g salted butter, diced
50 g honey

Faux caramel layer

90 g pitted dried dates
70 g pitted fresh medjool dates
180 g (¾ cup) peanut butter
50 g seed butter (a mix of tahini and pumpkin seed butter)
150 ml rice malt syrup

Chocolate layer

100 g dark chocolate (90% cocoa), broken into pieces
60 g honey
1 tbsp coconut oil
fleur de sel, for sprinkling

Preheat the oven to 160°C fan-forced. Line a 28 cm × 22 cm rimmed baking tray.

To make the base, pulse the ground almonds, flour and cinnamon in a food processor to combine. Add the butter and honey and pulse until the mixture just comes together.

Turn the mixture out onto the prepared tray. Fill a mug with boiling water. Heat a tablespoon in the water. Spread the mixture out evenly, using the back of the hot spoon. Reheat the spoon intermittently, so the mixture won't stick to it. Bake in the oven for 15 minutes or until just golden brown. Set aside to cool completely.

For the faux caramel layer, process the dates in a food processor until finely chopped and starting to stick together. Add the nut and seed butters and rice malt syrup and process on high speed until it forms a smooth mass. Spread the mixture evenly over the base. Use the backs of your fingers to press down, then smooth it out using the back of a spoon.

For the chocolate layer, melt the chocolate, honey and oil in a bowl set over a saucepan of simmering water, ensuring the water does not touch the bottom of the bowl, stirring continuously. Once combined, pour the chocolate evenly over the caramel layer. Sprinkle with fleur de sel. Refrigerate until the chocolate layer has completely set, about 45 minutes.

Working quickly, turn the slice out onto a large board and cut into 40 bars. Store in the fridge for several months.

COOK'S NOTES: *You can make these over 2 days – the base on the first day, the rest on the next day.*

CELEBRATING EASTER

'After the egg hunt, we start preparing the food. First, we roll out the yeast dough I prepared in the morning, smear on the chocolate filling and then braid the delicious Easter bread. We eat it warm out of the oven, ripping off large chunks.'

Easter can be one of those holidays that just falls away without being celebrated meaningfully. A couple of public holidays and a frenzied Easter egg hunt can be all that we do to mark the occasion. But unlike Christmas, with its retail-mad December lead-up and the general business of coming to the end of a year and desperately needing a break, Easter has a slower pace. Perhaps because of that I've turned to it over Christmas in some ways. While there isn't the excitement of presents for the kids, they do really enjoy the way we have come to celebrate Easter: with crafting, collecting, cooking and baking, and with chocolate eggs, of course.

In most of Europe, crafting with kids to the rhythm of the seasons is a constant. Even now, at the German school that my girls attend, the kids are always making something related to the time of year. And they always bring home an Easter art project. We make bunnies with pompoms, craft window decorations with translucent paper, and every year we make an *Osterstrauß* (Easter branch), the central focus of the decorations.

Traditionally, branches of fruit trees, such as cherry, birch and forsythia, are brought into the house a few days before Easter to encourage the blossoms to bloom in the warmth. They are placed in a large vase and eggs that have been painted and collected over the years are hung on the branches. Each year we add to these, and I rummage through organic shops and markets trying to find eggs with white shells, or as light as possible. I'll buy two dozen and over the weeks prior to Easter, carefully puncture both ends of the egg with a needle to form two holes, each one 2–3 mm in diameter. Then, I will blow on the one side, my face turning red, to remove first the egg white, then the more tricky egg yolk. With the eggs I make pancakes (page 218), French toast, fried rice or any other dish I can add scrambled egg to. The shells will dry out in the carton until it's time to decorate them.

Making the *Osterstrauß* takes about half a day. We start by taking our dachshund, Pretzel, for a walk down to Merri Creek, and on the way home we look for blue gum trees, our chosen branches for the *Osterstrauß*. We strip the leaves off the bottoms of the branches and place them in a big vase. Then, we adorn these with a selection of keepsake eggs from previous years. The kids love to remember who did what, and I often think I should add a little date stamp to these with an initial.

Then comes the fun part of adding new eggs to the *Strauß*. We spend hours chatting, being creative and complimenting each other's ideas. I have egg dyes sent over from Germany by relatives every year and the range, which used to be just the colours of the rainbow, has now grown to all sorts of fancy new techniques and colours. The best brand is Hartmann, should you want to try to find an online supplier. It is also completely fine to use a kid's paint set or acrylic paints to decorate the eggs. Textas, Sharpies and crayons all work. It's about letting your creativity flow, experimenting with different patterns, colours and techniques, and spending time together. If you ask the kids what they remember about Easter, other than the egg hunt, they will say the egg decorating!

My job is making the hanging device for each egg. It's fiddly. I take a match and break it in half, cut a 30 cm piece of sewing yarn in a colour that complements the egg, and tie it securely around the match. Now, I fiddle the small piece of wood through the top hole of the egg, until it drops into the shell with the yarn tied tightly onto it. It is with this that we hang the egg on the branches. We do this a week or two before Easter, so that we can enjoy the *Osterstrauß* for as long as possible, before packing it up after Easter.

On Good Friday, I observe my grandmother's ritual of not eating meat. For me, it is not so much a religious act as it is paying respect to my grandmother's strong Catholic faith. I think it is also good practice to eat less meat and to make a sacrifice sometimes.

Easter Sunday is the most fun day. The night before, when the kids are sleeping, I cut a bunny paw stencil from cardboard and, with the flour sifter loaded, I create some cute paw prints around the garden and street paths. The next morning, I wake up early, make myself a much-needed coffee and start hiding eggs near the paw prints and around the garden. At this time, I also make a quick yeast dough, which is for the Chocolate Easter Braid (page 206) that we will make together later in the day.

When the kids wake up they are straight out of the door, their mushroom-foraging baskets in hand, this time to be filled with enough chocolate to last a whole year. Their joy and surprise is so special and I'm proud to have put in the effort to enable this. Before kids, I'd often create an elaborate treasure hunt for the adults. It was so much fun and perhaps, as the kids grow into teenagers, it is something we will come back to.

After the egg hunt, we start preparing the food. First, we roll out the yeast dough I prepared in the morning, smear on the chocolate filling and then braid the delicious Easter bread. We eat it warm out of the oven, ripping off large chunks. At school, Maria and I had to do deportment and grooming as a subject, and, well, you don't cut bread at the table, it's always broken! Etiquette … it's fitting that we remember this, especially on Easter Sunday.

For lunch we set the table with thought and care and sit together as a family to share a meal. Mum usually joins us, too. It is often slow-roasted lamb with roast vegetables and delicious sauces. Nothing fancy, nor overly formal, just a meal that is conducive to spending time together. There is a fun game we play called *Eierditschen*, where you each have a hard-boiled egg that has been decorated. You hold it horizontally with the pointy end ready to face the egg of the opponent sitting next to you. You do a countdown, *eins, zwei, drei*, and then tap the eggs together, hoping the other person's egg cracks and not your own. The last one with an intact egg wins and, for us, it's just for bragging rights.

Religious or not, Easter is a good pausing point to be creative, to celebrate family and come together over a shared meal.

– Eva

Pancakes with Better Nutella

EIERKUCHEN MIT GESUNDER NUTELLA

After blowing out so many eggs to be decorated for the Easter branches, this is a great recipe to use up some of them. These pancakes are delicious and the kids love rolling them up and getting creative with other toppings. My kids love Nutella and none of the store-bought healthy options have been a substitute they're happy with, so we created one together that they devour. – ***Eva***

SERVES 4
Vegetarian

- 4 eggs
- 400 ml full-cream milk
- 250 g (1⅔ cups) plain flour
- 100 ml sparkling water
- ¼ tsp fine Himalayan pink salt
- ¼ tsp white sugar
- oil, for frying

Better Nutella

- 250 g hazelnut butter
- 2 tsp cold-pressed oil (macadamia oil is great)
- 50 g dark chocolate (50–70% cocoa), coarsely chopped
- 2 tsp Dutch-processed cocoa*
- ¼ tsp ground cassia*
- ¼ tsp ground wattleseed*
- ½ tsp coconut sugar*
- ⅛ tsp fine Himalayan pink salt

Cinnamon sugar

- 80 g (⅓ cup) white sugar
- ½ tsp ground cassia

SPICE SHORTCUTS*
3 tsp Gewürzhaus Feel Good Hot Chocolate

To make the better Nutella, combine all the ingredients in a saucepan (ideally with a spout) over medium–low heat and, stirring occasionally, heat until the chocolate is melted.

Pour the warmed mixture into a 300 ml sterilised glass jar (see page 29 for instructions) and spoon any excess into your mouth! Set aside.

Preheat the oven to 100°C fan-forced.

To make the pancakes, mix the eggs, milk, flour, water, salt and sugar in a bowl until smooth. Rest in the fridge for 15 minutes.

Heat a little oil in a large, non-stick frying pan over medium heat. Add a ladle of pancake mixture and swirl it around the pan to form a thin, even layer. Cook for 1–2 minutes, until the underside is golden, then flip and cook for a further minute until golden. Transfer to a plate in the warm oven and continue to cook the pancakes until all the mixture is used up.

To make the cinnamon sugar, mix the ingredients together in a small bowl.

Serve the pancakes with the better Nutella or cinnamon sugar.

COOK'S NOTES: *The better Nutella is gluten free, and you can use any nut butter for it: almond butter, ABC, cashew butter and peanut butter are all delicious. Any leftovers will keep in a sealed jar in the fridge for up to 6 months.*

REMEMBERING SOMEONE

'Later in her life, when Babi was a grandmother, she taught her skill to her granddaughter, a willing apprentice and someone to carry on her work. *Kipferl* were her love song. They helped her tell her story.'

There are certain people in our lives who are known for cooking or baking a particular thing. Maybe it's a Christmas pavlova or some cheese and oat biscuits for which nobody else knows the secret ingredient. Or maybe it's a spectacular lamb roast that is requested over and over again for family dinners. Whatever it is they make, it doesn't change over time and it is made regularly.

Our great-aunt Babi was one of these people and her signature dish was *Salzkipferl* (page 224). She made these for every family function, for every birthday – for every occasion, really. If you visited her, she would have *Kipferl* coming out of the oven. If you visited her at her daughter's house, she would still have a batch of freshly baked *Kipferl* ready for eating. She would pack up little bags of *Kipferl* if she went to someone else's house as a gift. We were sent back to Australia with little pouches of *Kipferl* for snacking on in the plane. This was always und unfailingly her offering.

As the youngest of all of the four children in her family, Babi was rarely in charge of anything when her sisters and their mother cooked or baked together in our Oma's apartment. Despite the fact she was in her sixties and seventies at this stage and more capable in the kitchen than most others, she would be relegated to tasks like beating eggs or grinding nuts. And she was even given feedback and commentary on her egg beating and nut grinding. It was a circle of harsh, uncompromising views in our great-grandmother's kitchen and Babi's opinions fell on deaf ears.

And so Babi wanted to make something of her own in the kitchen, something that she made better than everyone else, something no one else perhaps made at all, and something she most definitely wasn't going to take feedback on. She found all of that in *Salzkipferl*. Exactly when her baking of *Kipferl* started, neither of us can remember. But for as long as we visited, Babi was baking *Kipferl*. And they were beautiful – light and fluffy, with just the right amount of egg wash and salt flakes on top. Always perfectly shaped and perfectly golden brown.

Babi always beamed when she presented her *Kipferl* – a big smile from ear to ear and an immense pride in the fruits of her labour. 'Look what I made', her face would say. And in that moment, she always seemed at her best. She was seen and heard by those who mattered most. Our father, perhaps her greatest *Kipferl* fan when we were kids, always sang her praises and this made her bake all the more. Later in her life, when Babi was a grandmother, she taught her skill to her granddaughter, a willing apprentice and someone to carry on her work. *Kipferl* were her love song. They helped her tell her story.

Now that Babi is gone, we remember her most fondly in those moments, a huge basket of *Kipferl* in her hands, radiating and belonging. Her spirit lives on in her recipe and when we make *Kipferl* now, she comes back into our hearts and into our hands as we roll dough and shape crescents. Sometimes we will take some *Kipferl* to Dad and there will follow a moment where we all hold Babi together in our thoughts. We remember her life and we remember the joy these little baked goods gave her.

Babi's Salted Crescents

BABIS SALZKIPFERL

Cooking with our great-grandmother Oma Rosa, grandmother Oma Liesel, great-aunt Tante Dori and other great-aunt Tante Babi in the tiniest kitchen in the tiniest apartment are some of my most cherished childhood memories, and baking these crescents takes me back to that special time. – ***Eva***

MAKES 24
Vegetarian

500 g (3⅓ cups) plain flour, plus extra for dusting

40 g fresh yeast

300 ml full-cream milk, warmed

1 tsp white sugar

1 tsp fine Himalayan pink salt

100 g salted butter, softened

2 egg yolks

extra-virgin olive oil, for coating the dough

Topping

3 tsp extra-virgin olive oil

1 egg yolk, lightly beaten

sea salt flakes, for sprinkling*

caraway seeds, for sprinkling*

SPICE SHORTCUTS*
Gewürzhaus Everything Bagel Spice

Place the flour in a mixing bowl and create a well in the centre. Crumble the yeast into the well and add half the milk, the sugar and salt. Gently mix together, incorporating a little of the flour as you go. Sprinkle a thin layer of flour over the mixture, cover the bowl with a damp tea towel and place in a warm spot for 20 minutes. After this time, the yeast should be bubbling. Add the remaining milk, the butter and egg yolks and mix with a fork, working from the inside out, slowly incorporating all the flour.

When too difficult to mix with the fork, use your hands to scoop up the dough from the outside and fold it into the centre. Once the dough starts coming together, turn it out onto a lightly floured bench and knead it into a soft dough, about 5–7 minutes. Continue adding a little flour while kneading, until it is not sticky. Form it into a ball.

Flour a clean bowl, lightly rub the dough in oil, then transfer to the bowl. Dust it with flour again, cover with a damp tea towel and place in a warm spot for 1 hour, or until doubled in size.

Preheat the oven to 200°C fan-forced.

When the dough is ready, turn it out onto a lightly floured bench and briefly knead. Cut the dough into three equal pieces. Roll out one piece into a 30 cm round and brush it with 1 teaspoon of the oil for topping. Cut this circle into eight equal pizza-shaped slices. Take one of these slices and, starting at the wide end, tightly roll it up. Gently pull the tip, then press it lightly down onto the rolled-up part to secure it in place. Shape the roll into a crescent, then place it on a lined baking tray. Repeat this with the other seven slices. Once complete, let them rest for a further 20 minutes. Repeat this process with the other two pieces of dough.

Brush the crescents with the egg yolk and sprinkle with salt and caraway seeds. Bake for 15 minutes or until golden brown. Eat fresh out of the oven.

Advent & Christmas

'Advent is a time of build-up, of looking forward, of anticipation and of ritual. It is a time of waiting – an act that builds longing and yearning and a fond predisposition towards that which one awaits. And even more than that, it's the communal waiting that makes the Advent period so special and different from other times of the year, like birthdays or weddings. We are united in our preparations for the coming festival, sharing in the rituals and rhythms that usher it in.'

A COLOURFUL PLATE TO CELEBRATE THE SEASON

'Almost every family home has a *Bunter Teller* on their table during this time. It is carefully curated and consists of *Plätzchen* (biscuits), nuts in their shell, chocolate in foil wrappers, marzipan and small mandarins.'

For many Germans, Christmas preparations start in early November, before the official commencement of activities on the first Advent day, the fourth Sunday before Christmas. These Advent Sundays, along with the ever-popular Advent calendars, provide a day-by-day, week-by-week countdown to Christmas Eve.

During the Advent season, houses, streets and towns across Germany are beautifully decorated with Christmas lights, figurines and wooden ornaments. Walking along a German streetscape, you will be greeted by soft candlelight beaming from the windows, which are decorated with wooden arches and hand-crafted *Fensterschmuck* (window decorations). There are wreaths hanging on doors and offerings of little potted Christmas trees as you approach a house. The Christmas markets come to life in the central square of most towns, the smell of mulled wine and candied nuts wafting from the beautifully decorated stalls. All of December feels like Christmas, and it feels wonderful.

There is a word for this season in German, *Vorweihnachtszeit*, which literally translates to pre-Christmas time. Here in Australia, it is more difficult to get into this Christmas spirit with the days long and the weather hot. We are more likely to be found at the beach or a pub than bundled up at home with a mug of festive Advent tea.

A central focus of the *Vorweihnachtszeit* is the *Bunte Teller*, the 'colourful plate', filled with all manner of delicious things. Almost every family home has a *Bunter Teller* on their table during this time. It is carefully curated and consists of *Plätzchen* (biscuits), nuts in their shells, chocolate in foil wrappers, marzipan and small mandarins. These are the traditional elements, though many families deviate from this and add other favourite sweets or baked goods. The *Plätzchen* are the most important part, with ideally about five different colourful biscuits to choose from. *Zimtsterne* (page 239), *Lebkuchen* (page 238) and *Vanillekipferl* (page 241) are non-negotiables for me, but there are hundreds of different regional and national biscuits to choose from. The idea is to have biscuits with different bases – a nut base, a butter base, a butterless base, a macaroon base – as well as different fillings or coatings, including chocolate, jam, icing sugar and glaze. Variety is the idea so that family and guests can choose their favourites and be mesmerised by the array.

Baking for the *Bunter Teller* starts in November because there is a lot to get through! Each batch of cookies is made en masse, with the recipes being doubled or tripled, usually starting with the cookies that last longest, like the *Lebkuchen*. They are then stored away in tins until required.

The other common thread in the *Bunter Teller* is the vessel. As early as 1880, beautiful and ornate paper plates were used to house the biscuits and other items, but now metal or ceramic plates with Christmas motifs are more common. The plate is filled with whatever combination is desired and it always looks irresistible. It is then placed on the main table for the duration of the Advent season. Daily replenishment from the back-up tins keep it looking tempting. The remaining piles of baked goods are given to visiting guests, to teachers and colleagues as thank-you gifts, and shared among friends and family. At times, it feels like a barter economy where biscuits are traded back and forth between households, the diversity of offerings on the home plate changing and increasing with each swap. Some families also have individual, smaller *Bunter Teller* awaiting each family member under the Christmas tree, and these are tailored with the individual's favourite treats. They are then enjoyed on Christmas Eve, as presents are unwrapped and carols sung. A lovely finale to the Advent season and something to enjoy for days to come.

– Eva

THE BUNTER TELLER

Christmas-Spiced Butter Biscuits from Lüneburg

WEIHNACHTS-HEIDESAND

When our mum was a kid, Sundays were excursion days. No washing, no cleaning – Sunday was a day of rest when the family would pile into our grandfather's *Opel Rekord* and head off to explore the surrounding region. One of their semi-frequent destinations was the Lüneburger Heide, an area with sandy soils, potato and asparagus farms, and pinky-purple flowering heath as far as the eye could see. Our grandfather was a keen historian and dragged his children through the heath in search of Hun graves and stone-aged tools. To keep them motivated, they were treated to *Butterbrote* (buttered bread) as well as the occasional *Heidesand* biscuit, textured like the ground under their feet, with coarse sugar sprinkled on top.

Heidesand is loved at Christmas time all over Germany. This recipe is made extra nutty with almonds, spices and buckwheat, and is gluten free. I always have a log of this, pre-cut, in the freezer, ready to pop in the oven for really quick shortbread. – ***Maria***

MAKES 28
Gluten free / Vegetarian

200 g unsalted butter, roughly diced, at room temperature

80 g raw sugar, plus extra for sprinkling

½ tsp vanilla extract

3 tsp ground cassia*

2 tsp ground coriander seeds*

½ tsp ground ginger*

¼ tsp ground nutmeg*

pinch of sea salt flakes

100 g (1 cup) ground almonds

150 g buckwheat flour

100 g arrowroot flour

SPICE SHORTCUTS*
1½ tbsp Gewürzhaus Christmas Cake & Pudding Spice

Cream the butter and sugar with electric beaters for about 2–3 minutes. Add the vanilla, spices and salt and mix them through. Add the ground almonds and beat them in to just combine. Fold the flours into the butter mixture.

Using your fingers, knead the mixture to bring it together into a dough, then turn it out onto a clean bench. Shape it into a log approximately 25 cm long. It may be crumbly – work it just enough so it comes together and you can shape it. Wrap and refrigerate for at least 1 hour.

Preheat the oven to 180°C fan-forced. Line a baking tray.

Carefully slice the log into 8 mm thick biscuits. Place the biscuits on the prepared tray and bake for 10–12 minutes, until golden brown. You can prepare another tray, or wrap the remaining uncooked biscuits up and freeze them for baking another time.

Remove the biscuits from the oven and immediately sprinkle with the extra sugar. Cool before serving. Store in an airtight container for several weeks.

CASSIA
CLOVE
NUTMEG
GINGER
CARDAMOM

Spekulaas Spiced Cookies

SPEKULATIUS KEKSE

These cookies are originally from the Netherlands and Belgium; they are thin, crispy and packed with a signature blend of spices. If you can find some stunning *Springerle* moulds, the cookies will look just as amazing as they taste. The moulds come in many different sizes, shapes and motifs. – ***Eva***

MAKES 25
Vegetarian

- 225 g salted butter, at room temperature
- 210 g caster sugar
- 2 tsp ground cassia*
- ¾ tsp ground coriander seeds*
- ¼ tsp ground cloves*
- ¼ tsp ground nutmeg*
- ¼ tsp ground ginger*
- ¼ tsp ground allspice*
- ¼ tsp ground cardamom*
- 3 tbsp full-cream milk
- 380 g (2½ cups) plain flour, plus extra for dusting
- ¼ tsp baking powder

SPICE SHORTCUTS*
1 tbsp Gewürzhaus St Nicholas Spekulaas Spice

In a mixing bowl and using electric beaters, cream the butter and sugar for about 5 minutes. Add the spices and mix them in, then pour in the milk, a little at a time, and mix well.

In another bowl, sift the flour and baking powder together. Add this to the creamed butter and mix until all the ingredients are fully combined and the dough is quite firm.

With floured hands, shape the mixture into a ball. Wrap it and place in the fridge for 1 hour.

Take the dough out of the fridge and allow it to come to room temperature.

Preheat the oven to 170°C fan-forced. Line a baking tray.

Flour a bench and a rolling pin. Roll the dough out to about 3–5 mm thick, then press into your chosen mould (see Cook's Notes), cutting off the excess dough around the edges. Re-roll the dough offcuts into more cookies until all the dough is used.

Place the cookies on the prepared tray and bake for 10 minutes. Remove from the oven and let cool for a minute, then transfer to a wire rack to cool completely.

Store in an airtight container for several months.

COOK'S NOTES: *To use wooden spekulaas moulds, lightly flour them and press a suitably sized piece of dough into them. Cut off the excess dough by holding a knife parallel to the mould and sawing it off.*

To use a rolling pin imprinted with a pattern, roll it over the pre-rolled dough to imprint the pattern, then cut out the shapes with a knife, pasta cutter or cookie cutters.

To use silicone moulds, pre-roll the dough, cut it to the correct size, insert it into the moulds and lightly press down. You can also bake them in the silicone moulds rather than turning them out.

If you do not have moulds, use cookie cutters. Brush the shapes with milk and sprinkle with almond slivers prior to baking.

CINNAMON STARS
(PAGE 239)

SPEKULAAS SPICED COOKIES
(PAGE 235)

VANILLA CRESCENTS
(PAGE 241)

GINGERBREAD COOKIE
(PAGE 238)

CINNAMON STARS
(PAGE 239)

SPEKULAAS SPICED COOKIES
(PAGE 235)

CHRISTMAS-SPICED BUTTER BISCUITS
FROM LÜNEBURG (PAGE 234)

Gingerbread Cookies

LEBKUCHEN

If there is one cookie you are going to make at Christmas time, surely it has to be the gingerbread cookie. Nothing says Christmas quite like it, with its signature fragrance of ginger, spices and honey. The warm dough is a dream to work with and very forgiving for little hands. This dough can be made a long time in advance and is often left to develop its flavours for many months before baking.

MAKES 45
Dairy free / Vegetarian

250 g honey

125 g caster sugar

125 g vegetable shortening (such as Copha)

500 g (3⅓ cups) plain flour, plus extra for dusting

25 g Dutch-processed cocoa

3 tsp ground cassia*

3 tsp ground coriander seeds*

2½ tsp ground star anise*

2½ tsp ground ginger*

1 tsp ground nutmeg*

1 egg, lightly beaten

1 tsp potash

SPICE SHORTCUTS*
3 tbsp Gewürzhaus Gingerbread Spice

Combine the honey, sugar and vegetable shortening in a medium saucepan over low heat. Stir until the shortening has melted and the sugar has dissolved – the mixture should be bubbling gently. Remove from the heat and allow to cool slightly, about 5 minutes.

Transfer the honey mixture to a large mixing bowl. Sift the flour, cocoa and spices into another bowl. If using bicarbonate of soda and baking powder instead of potash (see Cook's Notes), add them now. Stir half the flour mixture through the honey mixture, then stir through the egg.

Dissolve the potash in 1 tablespoon of water in a small bowl, stirring until clear. Add this to the dough and mix until incorporated. Add the rest of the flour mixture, bit by bit, until the dough comes together.

Turn the dough out onto a lightly floured bench. Knead it gently for a few minutes until the mixture loses its stickiness. Add a little more flour if needed – the dough should be easy to knead. Shape it into a flat disc, place in a ziplock bag and chill in the fridge for about 1 hour.

When you are ready to roll out the dough, preheat the oven to 180°C fan-forced. Line two baking trays.

Roll out the dough on a lightly floured bench to about 5 mm thick. If the dough is too firm, leave it for a few minutes to soften. Cut out shapes using cookie cutters, re-rolling the dough until it is all used. Place the shapes on the prepared trays.

Bake for 8 minutes or until lightly browned. Transfer to a wire rack to cool. Store in an airtight container for many months.

COOK'S NOTES: *Potash is a raising agent used for heavy, honey-based doughs. It pushes the dough out rather than up and gives a better result with gingerbread. Potash is available from specialty stores, including Gewürzhaus; if you can't find any, replace it with 1 tsp each of baking powder and bicarbonate of soda.*

Cinnamon Stars

ZIMTSTERNE

Zimtsterne are one of the most popular Christmas cookies in Germany and they will be represented on almost every *Bunter Teller*. They are delicious: chewy, soft, a little crunchy, sweet and, generally, gluten free. The dough can be a little sticky and difficult to work with, but it's well worth the effort. – ***Eva***

MAKES ABOUT 50
Gluten free / Dairy free / Vegetarian

3 egg whites

pinch of fine Himalayan pink salt

220 g icing sugar, sifted, plus extra for dusting

3 tsp ground cassia

450 g (4½ cups) ground almonds

Glaze

1 egg white

pinch of fine Himalayan pink salt

100 g icing sugar, sifted

Place the egg whites and salt in a bowl and beat with electric beaters until soft peaks form, then start adding the icing sugar, a couple of tablespoons at a time. Continue to beat until all the sugar is incorporated and the mixture is thick and glossy. Add the cassia and ground almonds and fold them into the mixture until a dough forms. Tightly wrap the dough and refrigerate for at least 2 hours.

Place the dough on a bench sprinkled with icing sugar. Using your hands, flatten the dough into a disc, sprinkle with icing sugar, then roll it out evenly to just under 1 cm thick, using a rolling pin. Cut out stars with a star-shaped cookie cutter (any size you like) and place them on a lined baking tray. Knead the leftover dough back into a ball, then repeat until it is all used up. If sticky, dust the rolling pin and cookie cutters with icing sugar also.

Preheat the oven to 120°C fan-forced.

To make the glaze, beat the egg white and salt. When soft peaks form, add the icing sugar and beat it until the mixture is glossy, about 2 minutes.

To glaze the biscuits, load up a small pastry brush or clean paint brush with icing, and paint it onto the biscuits, starting in the centre. Tilt the brush sideways and trace the edges of each biscuit, dragging the icing from the inside out. The aim is to use as much icing as possible without it running over the sides of the biscuits.

Bake the biscuits in the oven for 20 minutes. The idea is to dry them out rather than bake them, making them deliciously chewy. Allow them to cool on the tray before eating. You can also leave them in the warm oven to cool down, which allows them to dry out a little more, making them extra chewy.

Once completely cooled, store in an airtight container for several weeks.

Vanilla Crescents

VANILLEKIPFERL

These moon-shaped cookies are not actually a German invention but rather originated in Vienna, Austria. Their buttery, nutty vanilla flavour and soft tenderness to bite make them a Christmas favourite throughout much of Europe. – ***Eva***

MAKES 25
Vegetarian

- 200 g (1⅓ cups) plain flour
- 80 g (¾ cup) ground almonds
- 150 g salted butter, at room temperature
- 80 g (⅔ cup) icing sugar, plus extra for dusting
- 1 egg yolk
- 1 vanilla bean, split and seeds scraped out
- ½ tonka bean, finely grated (optional)

In a mixing bowl, combine the flour, ground almonds and butter, rubbing the mixture with your fingers, working it until it resembles coarse breadcrumbs.

Add the sugar, egg yolk, vanilla seeds and tonka bean (if using) and repeat the process of rubbing the ingredients in with your fingers until combined and well blended.

Tip the dough onto a lightly floured bench and start kneading it. After about 2–3 minutes, the ingredients will come together and form a smooth dough. Divide it in half, then roll it into two logs, approximately 4 cm in diameter. Wrap them and refrigerate for 30 minutes.

Preheat the oven to 160°C fan-forced. Line a baking tray.

Remove the dough from the fridge. Pinch off walnut-sized pieces, roll them into little logs about 5 cm long, then taper the edges by rolling them a little thinner. Carefully bend into a crescent and place on the prepared tray.

Bake for 12 minutes or until they are just starting to colour. Remove from the oven and let them cool for a minute, then transfer the crescents to a wire rack. Immediately sift over a generous amount of icing sugar while they are still hot.

Cool completely and store in an airtight container for up to 1 month.

COOK'S NOTES: *You can replace the ground almonds with another nut meal, such as hazelnut or pistachio. The tonka bean is optional, but it gives a stronger almond/marzipan taste, which feels even more like Christmas.*

CINNAMON
WATTLESEED
VANILLA
ALLSPICE

Flourless Hazelnut Cookies with Wattleseed & Cherry

KIRSCH-HASELNUSSMAKRONEN MIT AKAZIENSAMEN

I love making these cookies. They came about by mixing and matching some of my favourite things: chocolate, hazelnuts and cherries. They require of the baker to cast aside some of the precision tools of today's trade and rather, to use their feeling and intuition. That's how we learnt to bake from our Oma and her sisters. Ingredient quantities were rarely used strictly, but rather as guidelines. Liquid was added only so far as the dough needed – no matter what the piece of paper said. It required them to pay close attention, to work the dough with their hands and *feel* when it was ready. I find this part of making these cookies so enjoyable. – ***Maria***

MAKES 28
Gluten free / Dairy free / Vegetarian

- 100 g hazelnuts
- 3 large egg whites
- 100 g runny honey
- ½ tsp vanilla extract or a knife tip full of vanilla seeds, scraped out of a vanilla bean
- 80 g ABC butter or almond butter
- ½ tsp roasted wattleseed
- ½ tsp ground allspice
- 1 tsp ground cinnamon
- 250–300 g ground almonds, plus extra
- 50 g block of dark chocolate (85% cocoa), cut into 28 × 1 cm squares
- 200 g cherry conserve or jam

In a heavy-based frying pan, roast the hazelnuts over medium–low heat until aromatic and the skins are cracking. Place in a clean tea towel and roughly rub off the skins. Cool, then finely grind in a food processor or nut mill. Set aside.

Preheat the oven to 160°C conventional. Line a baking tray.

In a large bowl and using electric beaters, beat the egg whites until stiff. Add the honey and vanilla and beat until glossy with soft peaks. Beat in the nut butter and spices, then fold in both nuts. Depending on the size of the eggs, you may need to add a little more or less ground nuts, so withhold some of them to start with. Keep adding ground almonds until the consistency of the dough is sticky and just workable. Don't overdo it, as the cookies will be less gooey if you add too much.

Shape the cookies by pinching off walnut-sized pieces of dough, rolling them into balls and placing them on the prepared tray. If your hands get too sticky, rub the dough off with some more ground almonds or with the back of a butter knife – a trick my great-grandmother always used. Similarly, if the dough gets too sticky, sprinkle some more ground almonds on top and it will be easier to roll.

Press down into each cookie with your finger to form a well – make sure the well's walls are intact. Place a piece of chocolate into each well, then add a dollop of cherry jam on top.

Bake for 20–25 minutes, until just turning golden. When you walk past the oven and can smell the cookies, they are ready. Cool completely before serving. They will keep in an airtight container for up to 10 days.

COOK'S NOTES: *These cookies get better with age, so make them ahead of time.*

THE MAGIC OF ADVENT

'It's the communal waiting that makes the Advent period so special and different from other times of the year, like birthdays or weddings. We are united in our preparations for the coming festival, sharing in the rituals and rhythms that usher it in.'

Christmas Eve is the most magical night of the year in our family. It's when we celebrate our German Christmas, continuing the traditions our mother cherished as a child. Our families come together in the late afternoon, the presents under the tree growing from a moderate assortment to an overflowing mass of colour, size and wrapping styles. The children are buzzing with anticipation, eagerly awaiting the annual arrival of the *Weihnachtsmann* (Santa Claus), checking out of the corners of their eyes through windows to catch a glimpse of his sleigh and reindeer. His imminent arrival remains imminent for far too long, and the children are restless, like concert-goers willing their idol to come on stage. Finally, one of the adults sights the sleigh flying past, and shortly after, the *Weihnachtsmann* arrives with a big knock at the front door, laden with a heavy sack and a *Rute* (switch), his hand-carved walking stick helping him to make his way into the midst of our company.

The children sit in front of the glowing Christmas tree, their little faces mesmerised by the theatre and the magic of the moment. Giddy with excitement, they wriggle around and hang on every word and gesture of the *Weihnachtsmann*. They pay extra attention when their name is read from his golden book, a report given on their behaviour and achievements in the year gone by. They each perform a song, receive a present and then the *Weihnachtsmann* departs, off to visit the next lot of children. It is a wonderful spectacle, enriching for all those involved and something we cherish all year.

Christmas Eve is the finale of the Advent season, before we head off to our Australian Christmases, where tables bow with turkey and puddings and brandy butter. Advent is a time that is celebrated somewhat haphazardly in Australia, but it's worthy of attention and consideration. Advent is a time of build-up, of looking forward, of anticipation and of ritual. It is a time of waiting – an act that builds longing and yearning and a fond predisposition towards that which one awaits. And even more than that, it's the communal waiting that makes the Advent period so special and different from other times of the year, like birthdays or weddings. We are united in our preparations for the coming festival, sharing in the rituals and rhythms that usher it in.

Like most, our children have Advent calendars, which they eagerly dash out to each morning to discover what's behind the next door. With their varying levels of understanding of time, the calendar helps them get a sense of how long it is until Christmas, and they share their countdown together.

Perhaps the most exciting day in the Advent period for the kids is *Nikolaustag* (Saint Nicholas Day). On the evening of 5 December, after spending a significant time cleaning and polishing their largest pair of boots, they each place one of their boots outside the back door in anticipation of the coming of Saint Nicholas overnight, who will fill their boots with chocolates, fruit and nuts, some lollies and a few small knick-knacks. There is much discussion during boot-cleaning as to what they might get this year, and excitement that Christmas is finally getting closer. The next morning, they race out to discover their boots filled with goodies and spend the next few days rearranging and eating their spoils.

Fairly early in the Advent period, we pull out all of the Christmas boxes and decorate the house with the varying collected items from past years of celebrating Christmas. There are things made by the children, pieces inherited, and decorations we have purchased on our travels and from our Gewürzhaus stores over the years: candle arches to sit on the fireplace or on a windowsill; pyramids with the Nativity scene, the spinning, hand-carved figurines powered by the heat of the candlelight; delicate little candleholders with Santas or angels or snowmen; garlands and window decorations. Opening these boxes is one of our favourite things and we look forward to this all year. We decorate slowly, with carols playing.

Finally, the Christmas tree goes up (page 267), its little lights putting us all in the Christmas mood more than anything else. Everyone gets involved in adorning the branches with treasured ornaments from the big box. When our mum was a child, the tree was brought in from the forest only on the morning of Christmas Eve. Our grandfather would painstakingly and meticulously balance out the pine branches by moving them where necessary. He would make a hole with his hand-drill and carefully place a sawn-off and sharpened branch into a space. In later years, this tradition went by the wayside as a more expensive blue spruce could be selected in the forest. Once his work was done, the family decorated the tree with real candles, sprinkled chocolate rings hung on ribbons, wooden baubles from our great-grandparents and, of course – a German Christmas tree of the 1950s and '60s wouldn't have been any other way – strands of delicate and glimmering soft white angels' hair, and shimmering silver or gold *Lametta* (tinsel).

What ties all of this together is the Advent wreath with its four candles, one for each Sunday preceding Christmas Eve. We light the first on the fourth Sunday before Christmas and continue to light an additional candle each Sunday until all four are glowing in our homes. We light them only on Sundays in our family; this helps us to be more mindful of slowing down in this hectic summer period. In Germany, the winter season slows things down naturally; the cold forces you inward and makes things feel cosy and *gemütlich* (page 176). In Australia, we really have to work at bringing this calm into the busiest time of year. And so, the Sunday lighting of the candles reminds us to slow down at least on this one day of the week, to bake cookies for our *Bunter Teller* (page 229), make salt dough decorations or craft window garlands with the kids, invite family or friends over to celebrate the season, and leave the pile of washing and the vacuuming till Monday. Something like a Sabbath, but with Christmas cookies, mulled wine and carols.

The celebration of Advent and Christmas is one of the most strongly held traditions that has endured into our modern society. We hold onto it because it brings, at least, moments of delight and joy and magic and a pause to our every day. It brings continuity and certainty – Christmas will come, every year, regardless of whatever else might come; there is a great deal of reassurance for our psyches in this rhythm.

Of course, there is the coming together of family – hopefully magical, sometimes not easy, always important. Because family is the stuff we are made of, family is one of the things we need to unrelentingly work on. Family, for many, is the mirror we hold up to ourselves. And at Christmas, everyone makes a little more effort than usual – shirts are ironed, hair combed back, a nice dress pulled out for the occasion. Everyone is on their best behaviour because that's what the occasion demands. We try a bit harder because, fundamentally, we all understand that sharing in celebration is something worth living for.

Christmas-Spiced Roast Duck

GEBRATENE WEIHNACHTSENTE

I used to cook duck a lot more: beautiful tender duck breasts with crispy skin, whole roast duck like this recipe or at one time, when I got into charcuterie, I even cured my own duck prosciutto, which turned out remarkably well. It really does feel a little more special and festive to cook a roast duck, especially during the Christmas season. – ***Eva***

SERVES 4–6
Dairy free

1 × 2 kg duck, neck and tail removed

1 lemon, quartered

5 garlic cloves, skin on and smashed

extra-virgin olive oil, to coat

Roast duck spice

¾ tsp ground yellow mustard seeds

½ tsp ground cassia

¼ tsp ground nutmeg

¼ tsp ground allspice

⅛ tsp ground cloves

⅛ tsp ground cardamom

3 tsp sea salt flakes

Sweet & sour marinade

2 tbsp brown sugar

2 tbsp maple syrup

2 tbsp apple cider vinegar

1 tsp soy sauce

1 tsp Dijon mustard

Preheat the oven to 180°C fan-forced.

Wash and pat the duck dry both on the inside and out. Score a diamond pattern into the duck breast, being careful to only score the fat and not the flesh. Prick the skin with a skewer or knife tip in all other areas except the legs. Place the lemon and garlic into the cavity, then fold the fatty bits on either side of the cavity over one another to close it. Take the legs and tie them together on the breast-side up, with kitchen string or foil.

To make the roast duck spice, combine all the ingredients in a small bowl. Generously coat the duck with oil, then rub the spice mixture over the whole duck evenly.

Place the duck, breast-side up, on a rack in a large roasting tin so the fat can drip off. Cook for 45 minutes, then turn the duck breast-side down. Cook for a further 30 minutes. During this time prepare the marinade by mixing all the ingredients together in a bowl.

When the 30 minutes are up, baste the duck with the marinade, then turn it back around with the breast facing up and baste this side too. Cook for another 40 minutes, basting once more with the remainder of the marinade halfway through the cooking time.

Rest the duck for 10 minutes before carving. Discard the lemon and garlic in the cavity before serving.

COOK'S NOTES: *The cooking time here is for a 2 kg duck and will need to be adjusted depending on the duck size. Allow 1 hour per 1 kg of duck and scale the cooking time accordingly. It's also a good idea to strain the duck fat during the cooking process if you want to keep it for future use or to add to your gravy. To make this recipe gluten free, use gluten-free soy sauce.*

Sweet & Sour Red Cabbage

ROTKOHLGEMÜSE

In Germany, this is a traditional side dish to any roast, commonly served at Christmas time and on Sundays for a more festive meal. The clove, juniper and bay give it that wintery feel, and the sweet and sour combination is simply delicious. – ***Eva***

SERVES 4–6
Gluten free / Dairy free

- 1 red cabbage (about 1.5 kg)
- 1 onion, finely diced
- 60 g duck fat
- 3 apples, peeled, cored and finely diced
- 7 cloves
- 7 juniper berries
- 3 dried bay leaves
- 5 tsp fine Himalayan pink salt
- freshly cracked black pepper
- 140 ml apple cider vinegar
- 2 tbsp white sugar

Remove the outer leaves of the cabbage, then quarter the cabbage and remove the core. Shred the quarters finely with a mandoline or, as our grandmothers did, cut it by hand (3–5 mm width is ideal).

In a large heavy-based pot, sweat the onion in the duck fat over low heat for about 5 minutes, or until translucent but not brown. Add the cabbage and 300 ml of water and carefully stir (note: the volume will quickly decrease). Cover with a lid and cook for 15 minutes.

Next, add the apple, spices, bay leaves, salt and a little pepper. Make a well and pour the vinegar and sugar into the fluid that has formed in the well. Cook for 1½ hours over low heat with the lid on, stirring carefully every 20–30 minutes.

Finally, taste and season again to your liking before serving – it should have a good balance of sour, sweet and salty.

COOK'S NOTES: *You can stud the cloves into a larger piece of onion so you can easily remove them at the end. Replace the duck fat with butter to make this dish vegetarian, or extra-virgin olive oil to make it vegan.*

Whole Baked Cauliflower in Sultana & Maple Syrup Sauce

GEBACKENER BLUMENKOHL MIT SULTANINEN-AHORNSIRUPSOßE

This cauliflower makes a lovely centrepiece for a special occasion. The complex yet mellow flavours and aromas of ras el hanout do the heavy lifting here and are combined with sultanas, maple syrup, lemon and butter in a delicious sauce.

SERVES 2–3
Gluten free / Vegetarian

- fine Himalayan pink salt
- 1 large cauliflower, about 25–30 cm in diameter
- 2 tsp ras el hanout

Sultana & maple syrup sauce

- 1¾ tbsp extra-virgin olive oil
- 2 tbsp sultanas, finely chopped
- 25 g salted butter
- 2 tsp ras el hanout
- finely grated zest and juice of ½ lemon
- 1 tbsp maple syrup
- ½ tsp fine Himalayan pink salt

Rose harissa yoghurt

- 2 tsp harissa spice mix
- 1 tsp rose petal powder
- 1 tbsp extra-virgin olive oil
- 250 g (1 cup) Greek-style yoghurt

Fill a large pot that will fit your cauliflower about half to three-quarters full with water. Add salt until the water is extremely salty to taste, then bring the water to the boil.

Make sure the cauliflower sits squarely on its base – if not, shave a little off the base to level it. Do not cut off the leaves – just trim the leaves at the top so the crown of the cauliflower is exposed.

Once the water is boiling, reduce the heat slightly, then add the ras el hanout and the cauliflower, upside down. Cook for 5–7 minutes at a rolling simmer – do not boil. Don't overcook: it should remain firm and not go soft. You are just giving it a small head start to soften it for the sauce to seep into later. Drain the cauliflower and let it cool for 20 minutes.

Preheat the oven to 220°C conventional. Grease a baking tray.

To make the sultana and maple syrup sauce, combine all the ingredients in a small saucepan over low heat and cook until the butter is melted. Stir briskly to thoroughly combine the ingredients.

Place the cauliflower on its base on the prepared tray. Slowly work the sauce into the cauliflower to cover it, rubbing it into the crevices. Also spoon some into the centre of the cauliflower, being careful not to break the florets. Bake for 30 minutes or until the cauliflower is brown – almost burnt – on top. Baste with the juices and bake for a further 5 minutes.

In the meantime, make the rose harissa yoghurt by combining the harissa spice mix and rose petal powder with 2 teaspoons of boiling water in a bowl. Stir, then set aside for 5 minutes. Add the oil and stir. Stand for a further 2 minutes. Add the yoghurt and stir well.

Serve the cauliflower hot with the yoghurt on the side. Store leftovers in an airtight container in the fridge for up to 1 week.

Tender Fennel Roast Pork with the Ultimate Crackling

FENCHEL SCHWEINEROSTBRATEN

Having a recipe for a fool-proof pork roast is a game changer. Especially one with a killer crackling, like in this recipe. The secret is in the preparation of the pork the day before, a hot oven and a good salt rub.

SERVES 6
Gluten free / Dairy free

1 × 1.8 kg free-range boneless pork shoulder roast, skin on, netting removed

Salt rub

3 tsp sea salt flakes*

1½ tsp crushed fennel seeds*

¼ tsp garlic powder or 1 garlic clove, crushed*

very finely grated zest of ¼ lemon*

pinch of freshly cracked black pepper*

SPICE SHORTCUTS*
5 tsp Gewürzhaus Crunchy Pork Crackling Rub

Put a full kettle of water on to boil.

Using a very sharp knife, such as a serrated kitchen knife, score the pork skin in thin strips, about 1 cm wide, all the way along and running down the sides of the roast. Cut right through the skin and into the fat layer, but not into the meat. Take your time with this step – it will pay off with amazing crackling!

Place the pork in a colander set in the sink. Slowly pour the boiling water over the skin. It should contract the skin between cuts. Remove from the sink and inspect the skin. If there are sections of your scoring that are not coming apart, you haven't scored deeply enough. Score these areas more deeply (but not through to the meat), then pour more boiling water on them. Remove from the sink and set aside to dry.

Make the salt rub by combining all the ingredients in a small bowl. Rub the mixture into the scored cuts of the skin, right into the cracks, all the way down the sides and across the top of the roast. Avoid leaving the rub on the skin as it will burn. Refrigerate, uncovered, overnight to dry the skin out. This yields a crunchier crackling.

The next day, remove the pork from the fridge and let it come to room temperature. Preheat the oven to 220°C fan-forced.

Place the pork – skin-side up and roughly shaped into a log – into a roasting tin. Roast the pork for 30 minutes, then reduce the temperature to 180°C and cook for an additional 15–20 minutes per 500 g of pork, depending on your oven. Remove the pork from the oven and rest, uncovered, for 15–30 minutes before serving.

COOK'S NOTES: *Choose a piece of meat with a thick skin and fat layer (ideally 1.5–2 cm). The fat keeps the roast moist and makes your crackling and roast more delicious. Get a larger piece of meat if you need – this recipe gives cooking times by weight, so is easy to adjust.*

Fig & Harissa Chutney

HARISSA FEIGEN-CHUTNEY

This chutney is made with just pantry ingredients, so you can whip up a jarful whenever the last one runs out. Its balance of sweet, acid and chilli matches well with a rich, fatty pork roast or pork belly.

MAKES 1 x 250 ML JAR
Gluten free / Dairy free / Vegan

- 100 g dried figs (about 5)
- 3 tbsp harissa spice mix
- 2 tsp rose petal powder
- ½ tsp sea salt flakes, plus extra if needed
- 2 tbsp extra-virgin olive oil
- ½ tsp red wine vinegar, plus extra if needed

In a food processor, blitz the figs until they form a smooth paste. Add the harissa, rose petal powder, salt and 120 ml of boiling water. Process until combined, then let the mixture infuse for 5 minutes. Add the oil and vinegar and blitz again. Season to taste with extra salt and vinegar, if needed.

Transfer to a sterilised jar (see page 29 for instructions) and store in the fridge indefinitely.

COOK'S NOTES: *If you don't have harissa in dried form, use an equal amount of paste, but add less water – go tablespoon by tablespoon until you reach a thick, chutney-like consistency.*

CLOCKWISE FROM TOP: TENDER FENNEL ROAST PORK (PAGE 256), FESTIVE FENNEL, APPLE & ALEPPO PEPPER SALAD (PAGE 260), FIG & HARISSA CHUTNEY (PAGE 257), CRUNCHIEST ROAST POTATOES (PAGE 261)

Festive Fennel, Apple & Aleppo Pepper Salad

FESTLICHER FENCHEL-APFELSALAT MIT ALEPPO PFEFFER

This salad is fresh and light and is always a crowd pleaser. You can mandolin the onion, apple and fennel bulb to make quick work of it, and pre-make the dressing if you need to throw it together just before your guests arrive. It's delicious with roasts, sausages, chicken and anything off the barbecue. – ***Maria***

SERVES 8–10 AS A SIDE
Gluten free / Dairy free / Vegan

- 1 red onion, halved
- fine Himalayan pink salt
- 1 small–medium fennel bulb
- 3 red apples, finely sliced
- 140 g lamb's lettuce or baby spinach, washed and patted dry
- 1 tbsp Aleppo pepper
- 2 tbsp dried barberries

Dressing

- 125 ml (½ cup) extra-virgin olive oil
- 3 tbsp white wine vinegar
- finely grated zest of 1 lemon
- 3 tbsp lemon juice
- 1 tsp sea salt flakes
- pinch of white sugar*
- pinch of freshly cracked black pepper*
- pinch of dried dill tips*
- 2 tbsp chopped chives*
- 1 tbsp chopped flat-leaf parsley*

SPICE SHORTCUTS*
1½ tbsp Gewürzhaus Salad Herbs

Finely slice the onion and place it in a small bowl. Add a few pinches of salt and toss it through, massaging the onion a little. Set aside.

Combine all the dressing ingredients in a jar and shake well. Set aside to infuse.

Remove the stems from the fennel bulb, then cut the bulb in half and finely slice. Place the fennel in a large mixing bowl and toss through the apple and lamb's lettuce. Squeeze a little of the excess liquid out of the onion, then add to the salad and mix thoroughly. Add the dressing and toss again.

Transfer the salad to a large serving plate and sprinkle with the Aleppo pepper and barberries.

COOK'S NOTES: *Lamb's lettuce, also known as corn salad or Rapunzelsalat, is used widely in Germany and I grow it every winter in my veggie patch. Plant it just once, then let it go to seed and you will be blessed with clumps of the delicious, buttery-smooth salad leaves all winter. Dried barberries are a tart, small berry and generally unsweetened. You could replace them with cranberries or currants, but reduce the amount slightly and try to find unsweetened ones. For the apples, pink lady are a good choice.*

Crunchiest Roast Potatoes

KNUSPRIGE RÖSTKARTOFFELN

Crunchy on the outside, soft and fluffy on the inside, garlicky and salty. These really are the perfect roast potatoes. I'm the master of shortcuts to minimise washing up, but in this case, even I succumb to the extra pot it takes to get these made; it really is worth it. – ***Eva***

SERVES 4
Gluten free / Dairy free / Vegan

- 3 tsp fine Himalayan pink salt, plus ⅛ tsp extra
- ½ tsp bicarbonate of soda
- 1 kg desiree potatoes, skin on, cut into thirds on an angle to maximise surface area
- 3 tbsp extra-virgin olive oil, plus extra if needed
- ½ tsp garlic powder*
- ¼ tsp sweet paprika*
- 1 tsp dried parsley*

SPICE SHORTCUTS*
2 tsp Gewürzhaus Garlic Lovers Spice

Adjust the oven rack to the centre position and preheat the oven to 240°C fan-forced.

Bring a large pot of water to the boil over high heat. Add the salt, bicarbonate of soda and potato and stir. Return to the boil, then reduce the heat to a simmer and cook until a knife easily pierces a potato chunk, about 10–15 minutes.

When the potato is almost cooked, combine the oil with the spices and extra salt in a small saucepan over medium–low heat and warm without burning the spices.

Turn off the heat, drain the cooked potato and leave to rest in the pot for 1 minute to allow any excess moisture to evaporate. Add the hot infused oil and toss to coat, shaking the pot roughly, until a layer of mashed potato–like paste has built up on the potato chunks.

Transfer the potato pieces to a large baking tray and spread out evenly. Roast without moving them for 20 minutes – opening the oven door every now and then for a few seconds releases the steam and makes them even more crunchy. Turn the potato, drizzle over a little more oil if required and continue roasting for 30 minutes or until the potato is deep brown and crisp all over. Serve immediately.

Store any leftovers in an airtight container in the fridge for several days.

COOK'S NOTES: *These are also delicious on their own with dollops of sour cream and generous spoonfuls of Crunchy Chilli Oil (page 34).*

Rum Plums

PFLAUMEN MIT RUM

If you have a plum tree, you have an annual need to do something with the bucketloads of fruit on your tree. This recipe came about from many seasons of making different things; one late night, we added a nip of rum to our bowls of stewed plums with dollops of vanilla yoghurt. We have never looked back. – ***Maria***

MAKES ABOUT 1 LITRE
Gluten free / Dairy free / Vegetarian

- 1 kg plums, stones removed, quartered
- ¼ tsp ground star anise
- ¼ tsp ground cinnamon
- pinch of dried thyme
- a few pinches of freshly cracked black pepper
- pinch of sea salt flakes
- 2 heaped tbsp honey, plus extra to taste
- 2–3 star anise
- about 2–3 tbsp good-quality dark rum

Place all the ingredients, except the whole star anise and rum, in a medium saucepan and stir. Gently heat over medium–low heat to a very low simmer and cook for about 15 minutes. Add more honey to taste.

Transfer the plum mixture to sterilised jars (see page 29 for instructions). Place a whole star anise on the top and add a swig of rum (about 1 tablespoon) before sealing. Heat-treat in a water bath at 90°C for 30 minutes (see page 29).

The plums will be most flavoursome after infusing for several weeks. Store in the pantry for 1–2 years. Once opened, store in the fridge for 2 weeks and make sure you use only a clean spoon to remove the plums, as the sugar content is low and mould will form more easily than in conventional preserves.

Serve either hot or cold, with a dollop of yoghurt or ice cream.

COOK'S NOTES: *If you don't want to preserve the plums, you can also use this recipe to make a batch to serve for dessert. Simply omit transferring the plums to jars and instead cool them in the pot or serve immediately. Add the rum to each portion at the table for some extra fanfare.*

Summer Berry Pudding with Vanilla Sauce

ROTE GRÜTZE MIT VANILLESOßE

This pudding is kind of like the German version of trifle. It looks beautiful and festive and can be served in a large glass bowl on the table for extra impact. I also really love making this in winter and eating it while still warm. – ***Eva***

SERVES 4
Vegetarian

- 600 g mixed frozen berries
- 1 x 400 g jar pitted morello cherries, drained, liquid reserved
- 410 ml cherry syrup (reserved from the jar above)
- 80 g (⅓ cup) white sugar
- ¼ tsp ground cassia
- 1 vanilla bean, split and seeds scraped out
- 60 g (½ cup) cornflour

Vanilla sauce

- 500 ml (2 cups) full-cream milk, plus 2 tbsp extra
- 1 tbsp white sugar
- reserved vanilla seeds (see above)
- 2 tbsp cornflour
- 2 egg yolks

Place the berries, cherries, 250 ml (1 cup) of the cherry syrup, sugar, cassia, vanilla bean and 250 ml (1 cup) of water in a saucepan over medium heat and bring to a simmer.

Mix the cornflour and remaining cherry syrup together until smooth, then slowly pour this mixture into the simmering ingredients in the pan, stirring vigorously with a whisk. Cook on a low simmer for 3 minutes. Remove from the heat and pour into individual glasses or one large glass bowl, leaving at least 1.5 cm at the top of the vessel. Refrigerate.

To make the vanilla sauce, heat the milk, sugar and reserved vanilla seeds in a saucepan over medium heat and bring to a low simmer. Place the 2 tablespoons of extra milk, the cornflour and egg yolks in a small bowl and mix until smooth. Slowly pour this mixture into the hot milk, whisking vigorously. Cook over low heat for 1 minute, whisking continuously.

Remove the puddings from the fridge, pour the vanilla sauce over top and serve warm or refrigerate until desired. This dessert is delicious served warm in winter and cool in summer.

Store any leftovers in an airtight container in the fridge for several days.

AN ALMOST-REAL CHRISTMAS TREE

'In those days we always had a real Christmas tree. Always. Having a real tree was – like Coco Pops for breakfast – something that was a given, the merits of it never discussed or second guessed.'

There is a picture book from our childhood that I read to my kids every Advent, about a little boy dressed from head to toe mostly in blue, who lives in a tiny village on the edge of a deep-green forest of fir, spruce and pine. His father is a forester, and every Christmas he prepares and transports the Christmas trees to the nearby town to be sold at the Christmas market. It's the story of the coming of Christmas, of making presents before they could be bought in department stores, of baking and decorating many, many biscuits in the warm kitchen with Mum and Grandma, of a place where snow falls thick and steadily all through December and where time is much slower than it is today.

The book ends with a short reflection that, every year, the forest comes into our homes with one tree, its green boughs shimmering in the soft candlelight that adorns it, the beautiful fragrance of spruce uplifting us, and that we value the light this tree brings into our home more than any ray of sunshine.

I love this book very much. It fills my boots with warm winter socks and is so life-affirming. It reconnects me to the Christmas of our childhood, where we also had snow piled up outside our mother's family home and our Oma's little apartment on the Steinberg, the places we celebrated Advent and Christmas every year during our long Australian school holidays.

In those days we always had a real Christmas tree. Always. Having a real tree was – like Coco Pops for breakfast – something that was a given, the merits of it never discussed or second guessed. The tree was always a beautiful fir or, if my mum got her way, a blue spruce – from the nearby forest, sold, as in the book, by the local forester. We would drive there in Dad's winter-tyred black Golf GTI. I remember the road we took, up past the *Ententeich*, snow covering everything around. Once selected, the tree was secured to the roof racks, skis pushed to one side, and off we drove. It was always a special trip.

Now, living in a very different time and place, having a real tree every year is something that I haven't come to terms with and something that I don't do. There are a few reasons. One, I am not a fan of the pine Christmas trees that are sold here. Nor is anyone in our family. We have been spoilt by the beautiful, deep blue-green and silver colours and the bushy, symmetrical branches of blue spruce and fir. Two, I struggle with the notion of adding more agricultural land, more pesticides and herbicides, to commercially grow something that we enjoy for such a short period of time. I think of the future of my children. Yet there is a paradox in this. In the book we read, the bringing in – the sacrifice – of the tree is the central, symbolic gesture of Christmas. It helps to bring the family, community and their natural surrounds together and to weave the fabric of their relations tightly. And that is the stuff that makes for a solid future of wellbeing for all involved, including the children.

One year I came up with a solution to my dilemma – one that brings much joy, fragrance and a real tree into our house, yet doesn't require the felling of a tree. Until the day when we have more land, when I will plant a small grove of spruce or fir, adding an additional tree every year, and until we can take that first tree and treasure it, this is what we will do.

The solution requires you to find the beautiful big fir, spruce, pine or cedar trees – anything that takes your fancy and has needles – around your neighbourhood or in your local parks and to then collect some of their branches to weave into your plastic tree.

Begin scouting a few weeks before you want to collect the branches. Look around as you walk, jog, drive – you will be surprised how many beautiful specimens are growing around you. Start in your own garden, then your neighbourhood and local parks or arboretums. If you spot something you like, take a few lemons from your garden or some homemade *Zimtsterne* (page 239), tuck this book under your arm and ring the doorbell of the tree's custodian. Explain what you are doing, show them the pictures in this book and offer your barter. You might make a new friend. Another place you can scout is on your local Facebook noticeboard. Put up a post saying you are looking for branches and offer your barter.

If you are collecting from your local parks, take a big, deep bag to disappear your branches into. There will be those among you who will say, 'But you are not allowed to remove things from parks!', and to you I will say, 'Yes, you are right'. And yet we have reached a time and place where blanket rules may no longer serve us or our environment. They probably never did. And so, I have made the judgement call that I would rather break the rules by removing a few branches of a big, old tree in our local arboretum – and only if I feel it will not harm the tree – than to cut down a whole tree in its place.

A few weeks before Christmas, set up your plastic tree in the usual way. (It can be handed down or used. It can be dodgy. Even short! We use a very old 1 metre Ikea tree that I bought in my uni days.) We do this on the third Advent, so that we have about two weeks until Christmas. As you will be weaving branches through the tree and they won't be in water, they will lose their needles if you do this too early.

Place a big piece of fabric underneath where you will position the tree, if you have carpet or floorboards with cracks – this will make the clean-up a lot easier. Spread the fabric out so that it covers about 50 cm more than the tree's diameter. Consider a box or similar underneath the fabric if you want to add some height to your tree. If you have a large tree, position it in its place. For a small or medium tree that you can easily move, you can weave and add the lights before you put it in place.

Next, go and collect your branches. Please do this with someone. Make it a ritual. In our family, I do this with my son, and my daughter is now joining the branch crew. We have a fairly established branch route and rhythm. The kids love this.

Select trees that are not too small or spindly. There are certain species that hold onto their needles for much longer than others, so experiment with different branches in the first year at least. I don't have answers to which species are better than others in this regard. Nor have I googled much. I'm sure you could. Or you could just be an adventurer and select those branches that speak to you and be okay with needles dropping.

Use a sharp pair of secateurs (kitchen shears will not do) to cut the branches to a length of about half the diameter of your tree. Make sure you cut on a slight angle and that you cut to a bud or lateral branch. A well-placed prune will encourage growth. Space out your branch removal if you are taking a few from one tree. How many branches you will need depends on how big and sparse your plastic tree is. We collect a decent bundle for our small tree, so you may need two big bundles for a large tree.

When you get home, put some Christmas carols on and adorn your tree. Starting at the bottom, place your collected branches between the plastic branches, cut-end first. If they are too long, remove and prune. Work around the tree, then up, shortening the branches as you need. For the top, reserve some soft, small-needled lateral branches.

Next, wrap the tree in a light chain, starting at the bottom. If you haven't already, position the tree. Then, decorate your tree. Take your time. Let the kids express themselves, even if it means there are five pink baubles hanging on one branch. Stand back and assess. Add some more ornaments where there are empty spots. Now add your tree topper.

Place any presents you have already wrapped under the tree and enjoy what you have created.

—

If you have any leftover branches, you can place them in a sturdy vase (add some gravel or sand to weigh it down if necessary). Add some small ornaments and decorate another corner of your house.

When Christmas is over, remove the branches from the tree. If you have a garden shredder or mulcher, you can mulch these and feed them to any acid-loving plants like blueberries, conifers or hydrangeas. We feed ours to the strawberry plants and to the little blue spruce growing in our front yard.

*– **Maria***

CLOVE
STAR ANISE
HIBISCUS
CINNAMON
CASSIA

Winter Warming Mulled Wine

GLÜHWEIN

The sweet smell of cinnamon, the warmth of your hands wrapped around your mug. For me, this is such a beautiful pausing moment in winter where you enjoy a glass of *Glühwein* together with friends. We make this a lot when we are skiing and it is more linked with winter than Christmas for me, although I do look forward to braving the German winter again and going to the *Weihnachtsmarkt*, the traditional Christmas market in the town square of our beloved UNESCO world heritage listed town of Goslar. – ***Eva***

SERVES 4
Gluten free / Dairy free / Vegan

1 bottle of red wine (merlot or cabernet sauvignon are great)

60 g sugar

5 cloves*

2 star anise*

½ tsp dried hibiscus flower*

1 cinnamon quill*

1 cassia stick*

1 orange, cut into slices

SPICE SHORTCUTS*
2 tsp Gewürzhaus Glühwein Gewürz, in an infuser bag

Place all the ingredients, except the orange, in a saucepan over low heat and gently warm for 15–20 minutes, being careful not to boil the wine. Strain and serve while hot with a slice of the orange in each glass or mug.

COOK'S NOTES: *If I have been baking a lot and have an empty pod from a split vanilla bean handy, I will add one to the mulled wine for a little extra flavour.*

—

Alcohol-Free Mulled Wine

To make an alcohol-free version, simply replace the red wine with 500 ml (2 cups) of clear apple juice, 200 ml of orange juice and 50 ml of blackcurrant juice. You can also tailor this to your child's favourite juice, fruit tea or a combination of both (you may just need to adjust the sugar). I prefer clear juices as the colour of the drink is nicer.

Schnaps, Two Ways

SCHNAPS AUF 2 ARTEN

Schnaps runs in the veins of all Germans. From north to south, there is no heavy meal that isn't punctuated by a nip of this wonderful digestive. Distilled with anything from nuts to fruit to herbs, *Schnaps* can be high or low proof – take your pick! Personally, I like the strong stuff – a high-quality, multiple-times-distilled *Schnaps* is smooth and life-affirming when you take a big swig. It warms the throat and then the tummy and makes me patriotically happy. *Prost!* – ***Maria***

THYME
TONKA
PEPPERBERRY

Cherry & Thyme Liqueur

KIRSCHLIQUEUR MIT THYMIAN

The word for medicinal herb in German is *Heilkraut,* translated as 'healing herb'. I love the boldness of this word and the reminder that the things that grow around us can heal us. I make this liqueur from the thyme growing in my garden, pollinated by the bees from our hive. The alcohol extracts all of the healing goodness from the thyme quite quickly – you will be surprised at its potency. Thyme is well known and widely used in cough preparations, so have a swig of this regularly when you are ailed by a cough. – ***Maria***

MAKES ABOUT 450 ML AT 20% ALCOHOL
Gluten free / Dairy free / Vegan

75 g (⅓ cup) raw sugar

200 ml pure sweet black cherry juice

1 tonka bean

6 pepperberries

2 short thyme sprigs

250 ml (1 cup) high-quality 40% spirit, such as *Korn* (see Cook's Notes on page 277) or gin

Dissolve the sugar in the juice, with the tonka bean and pepperberries, in a saucepan over low heat. Cool completely.

Place the thyme in a 750 ml glass bottle. Add the spirit. When the sugar syrup is cool, add it to the bottle and swill to mix. Make sure the thyme is submerged. Steep for 2 days or until the liqueur is infused to your liking.

Strain the liquid into a decorative bottle and place the whole ingredients in the compost. You can also remove ingredients when they have infused enough – leave the pepperberries and tonka bean for longer than the thyme, if you like.

Store indefinitely in your drinks cabinet.

COOK'S NOTES: *Look in health-food stores for the pure cherry juice. It needs to be preservative and sugar free, as well as heat-treated. Alternatively, you can juice your own cherries if you have a tree.*

VANILLA
CINNAMON
STAR ANISE
CLOVE
CARDAMOM

Spiced Christmas Schnaps

WEIHNACHTSSCHNAPS

This *Schnaps* is an ode to the flavours of Christmas. Enjoy it in a pretty little glass after eating a big piece of gingerbread or any other cake, at any time of the year! We love to drink it when playing cards.

MAKES ABOUT 250 ML (1 CUP) AT 35–38% ALCOHOL
Gluten free / Dairy free / Vegetarian

- 1 cinnamon quill
- 1 cassia stick
- 8 star anise
- 2 cloves
- 5 cardamom pods, bruised
- peel of 1 orange, sliced and without pith
- 250 ml (1 cup) high-quality 37–40% spirit, such as *Korn* or gin
- 1–2 heaped tsp runny raw honey
- ½ vanilla bean, split and seeds scraped out

Place the spices and orange peel into a glass bottle that will hold at least 300 ml. Add the spirit and shake. Close the lid and leave the spices to infuse for 2–4 days. Taste daily to see when you are happy with the infusion. The longer you leave the infusion, the more the anise flavour will develop from the star anise.

Strain off the liquid, put the whole ingredients in the compost and return the infused spirit to the bottle.

Add the honey to the bottle, depending on your taste, and shake vigorously to dissolve it, about 2 minutes. Add the vanilla bean and seeds and swill the bottle to disperse the seeds. Let this infuse for at least another week before serving. You can then either remove the vanilla bean or leave it to continue infusing.

Store indefinitely in your drinks cabinet.

COOK'S NOTES: Korn *is a popular German white spirit made from fermented grain and is commonly used to make* Schnaps *infusions.*

Conversion Charts

Measuring cups and spoons may vary slightly from one country to another, but the difference is generally not enough to affect a recipe. All cup and spoon measures are level. One Australian metric measuring cup holds 250 ml (8 fl oz), one Australian metric tablespoon holds 20 ml (4 teaspoons) and one Australian metric teaspoon holds 5 ml. North America, New Zealand and the UK use a 15 ml (3-teaspoon) tablespoon.

LENGTH

Metric	Imperial
3 mm	⅛ inch
6 mm	¼ inch
1 cm	½ inch
2.5 cm	1 inch
5 cm	2 inches
18 cm	7 inches
20 cm	8 inches
23 cm	9 inches
25 cm	10 inches
30 cm	12 inches

LIQUID MEASURES

One American pint = 500 ml (16 fl oz)
One Imperial pint = 600 ml (20 fl oz)

Cup	Metric	Imperial
⅛ cup	30 ml	1 fl oz
¼ cup	60 ml	2 fl oz
⅓ cup	80 ml	2½ fl oz
½ cup	125 ml	4 fl oz
⅔ cup	160 ml	5 fl oz
¾ cup	180 ml	6 fl oz
1 cup	250 ml	8 fl oz
2 cups	500 ml	16 fl oz
2¼ cups	560 ml	20 fl oz
4 cups	1 litre	32 fl oz

DRY MEASURES

The most accurate way to measure dry ingredients is to weigh them. However, if using a cup, add the ingredient loosely to the cup and level with a knife; don't compact the ingredient unless the recipe requests 'firmly packed'.

Metric	Imperial
15 g	½ oz
30 g	1 oz
60 g	2 oz
125 g	4 oz (¼ lb)
185 g	6 oz
250 g	8 oz (½ lb)
375 g	12 oz (¾ lb)
500 g	16 oz (1 lb)
1 kg	32 oz (2 lb)

OVEN TEMPERATURES

Celsius	Fahrenheit
100°C	200°F
120°C	250°F
150°C	300°F
160°C	325°F
180°C	350°F
200°C	400°F
220°C	425°F

Celsius	Gas mark
110°C	¼
130°C	½
140°C	1
150°C	2
170°C	3
180°C	4
190°C	5
200°C	6
220°C	7
230°C	8
240°C	9
250°C	10

Thank You

To Mama – thank you for nurturing us and giving so much of yourself to raising us. You fostered our imaginations, supported our ventures and have been there for us unwaveringly. We are lucky to have you as our Mama and the kids as their Oma. I (Eva) have my openheartedness, ability to connect, love and generosity from you. I (Maria) am grateful for your big heart, your vulnerability and your love of life.

To Oma – we have so many special memories with you, Oma. You were and remain such an important part of our lives. You gave us time, wisdom, belonging, unconditional love and patience; our relationship with you was like no other. Losing you was devastating but we feel you guiding us and know that what you instilled in our young hearts will always remain. With this book, we honour you and share what you taught us with our children and their families to follow.

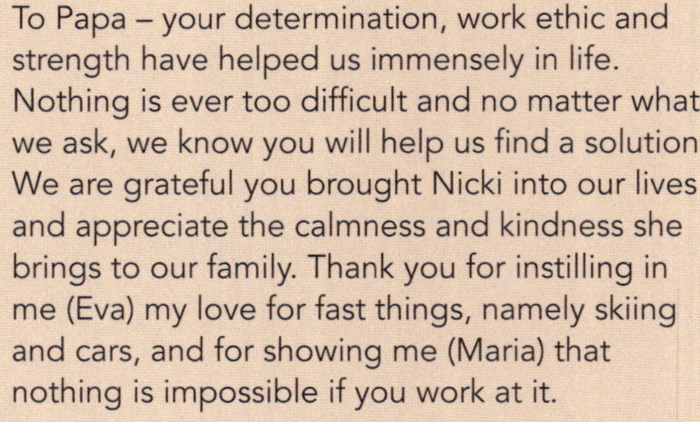

To Papa – your determination, work ethic and strength have helped us immensely in life. Nothing is ever too difficult and no matter what we ask, we know you will help us find a solution. We are grateful you brought Nicki into our lives and appreciate the calmness and kindness she brings to our family. Thank you for instilling in me (Eva) my love for fast things, namely skiing and cars, and for showing me (Maria) that nothing is impossible if you work at it.

To Isabella and Sebastian – the best part of our unconventional family is the both of you. We will always protect and love you.

To everyone from Gewürzhaus, especially Grant – a heartfelt thank you. Each and every one of you puts so much of yourselves into your work, and through that, we have created something magical that nurtures and inspires so many people. Thank you for caring; thank you for showing up for all these years. We would not have written this book without you.

To everyone who worked on this book – Mary, Jane, Michelle, Ariana, Megan, Helena, Armelle, Deb, Meryl, Sarah, Chris, Amy, Mum and all of the others behind the scenes – you are all artists in your own right and we are so very grateful to have had your skilled hands helping us throughout this process. Mary, you shared our vision for this book right from the start and you took a leap of faith – for that, we are truly grateful. Jane, you have been so kind and patient. It's been a pleasure getting to know you. Michelle, thank you for your lovely designs. Armelle, Deb, Meryl, Sarah, Chris and the studio crew, thank you for your hard work and perfectionism. You have all contributed to the recipe photography exceeding our wildest dreams. Finally, a huge thank you to Amy, the first and only photographer at Gewürzhaus – you give us so much more than pictures. You have inspired this book from the very start. Thank you for believing in us and helping us to express our way of cooking and ritualing so wholesomely.

MARIA:

To my love hearts, Benjamin and Matilda, for growing the size of my heart infinitely. You have shown me the world all over again and I love you fiercely. I am so grateful to be your mother; know that I am always with you, no matter where we each find ourselves. Bennie, when you came into my arms, you healed something in me I didn't even know was broken. You are gentle, kind and strong, and I am so, so proud of you. Tildy, you are my little ray of sunshine. Your fierce sense of self and joy in life are so deeply nourishing. I know you will hold a mirror up to me when no one else will dare; I hope I will honour your strength when you do.

To Gordon, for everything. You are my steady state and my love for you grows with every year we are together. Thank you for lightening the load, for opening your heart, for your humour when our little family needs it the most, and for always and unfailingly supporting me. Our relationship has taught me more than any other has; thank you for showing up, again and again, for the ride.

To Eva, for the many years we have been touring this thing called life together – as sisters, as business partners and now, as authors. Your drive, determination and spirit have pushed me ahead so often. We used to tell people that we balanced each other out at work; I've come to understand that we do that in life, too. Thank you for not giving up on me as we've navigated those balances. I love you so much.

To Maddy, Doug, Leah, and especially Nic and Ann, for accepting me so gracefully and wholeheartedly into your family. You are the best kind of people and I'm so very lucky to have you. Ann, to you especially, for feeding, nurturing and celebrating us with so much love and spirit.

To Jan, for shining your light. You helped me find my way around in the dark and then far beyond. This book is in no small part thanks to your unwavering love and courage.

EVA:

To meine kleinen Engelchen, Romy und Nina. You both will remain the best life choice I ever made. I am honoured to be able to guide you through life, to show you love and affection, to instil in you our values, culture and heritage through my thoughts and actions. Romylein, your ability to understand people, see different perspectives and repair in conflict has taught me so much; you are magical and wise beyond your years. Your empathy and kind heart are a true gift. Ninchen, you will always be my little one. You are fiercely protective of the ones you love, strong in every sense of the word and tender with the ones you hold closest. I can't wait to see where life takes you both and wish that you will always be there for one another. I hope you never stop telling me, '*Mama, zu viele Küsschen*'. *Ich liebe euch über alles.*

To Ia, without you we wouldn't be where we are in Gewürzhaus and this not-so-little passion project would also not be created. You've always been my big sister and guided me along in life and I'm grateful for your vision, determination and big-picture thinking. Thank you for putting so much effort, thought and love into what you do. What we have created here will be cherished for life.

Index

D

E

O

P

R

S

Pan Macmillan acknowledges the Traditional Custodians of country throughout Australia and their connections to lands, waters and communities. We pay our respect to Elders past and present and extend that respect to all Aboriginal and Torres Strait Islander peoples today. We honour more than sixty thousand years of storytelling, art and culture.

A Plum book

First published in 2023 by
Pan Macmillan Australia Pty Limited
Level 25, 1 Market Street,
Sydney, NSW 2000, Australia

Level 3, 112 Wellington Parade,
East Melbourne, VIC 3002, Australia

Design by Michelle Mackintosh
Typesetting by Megan Ellis
Editing by Ariana Klepac
Index by Helena Holmgren
Photography by Armelle Habib, except for images on pages 2, 6, 8, 9, 12, 20, 25, 26, 28, 35, 57, 71, 86, 89, 92, 93, 118, 121, 132, 135, 136, 137, 139, 143, 150, 212, 215, 216, 231, 244, 248, 266, 270, 279 and 280 by Amy Whitfield, and images on pages 50, 53, 99 (top), 197, 223 and 281 courtesy of Maria and Eva Konecsny
Prop and food styling by Deb Kaloper
Food preparation by Meryl Batlle, Sarah Watson, Chris Yuille, and Maria and Eva Konecsny
Ritual styling on pages 2, 6, 12, 20, 25, 26, 28, 35, 57, 86, 89, 92, 93, 118, 121, 132, 135, 136, 137, 139, 143, 150, 212, 215, 216, 231, 244, 248, 266, 270, 279 and 280 by Maria and Eva Konecsny
Colour reproduction by Splitting Image Colour Studio
Printed and bound in China by 1010 Printing International Limited

A CIP catalogue record for this book is available from the National Library of Australia.

10 9 8 7 6 5 4 3 2 1

German-born sisters, Maria and Eva Konecsny, founded Gewürzhaus in 2010 when they opened their self-scoop spice store in Melbourne, the first of many across Australia. Gewürzhaus blends and mills more than 100 exclusive spice seasonings, and sells an extensive range of single-origin spices from around the world.

For Maria and Eva, cooking from the home and heart has always been an integral part of connecting four generations of women in their family. They carry on these traditions and rituals with their own families in Victoria, Australia.

gewurzhaus.com.au